The Millionaire Maker

John and Ananda McIntosh

ISBN: 978-1434839282

Published by: Inner Scape Productions
In association with: Create Space
Printed in: The United States of America

Disclaimer

The opinions expressed in this book are of the authors' and while partially inspired by their relationship with Herbalife and Mark Hughes, in no way are meant to claim that they are the words, thoughts, actions, opinions, teachings or policy of Herbalife International, Mark Hughes of the Mark Hughes Estate.

Drawing by: John McIntosh

Contents

GRATITUDE

LOVE & COMPASSION

WORLD SERVICE

THE NEXT STEP

THE INSIDE PLAN

Introduction

The Basic Thread There is a basic thread that winds its way around and through every aspect of life in the human drama. This thread is like a DNA signature that carries with it the Universal Principles for Infinite Supply. We have all felt its influence in the hundreds of little things we do each day. In each and every tiny success we achieve from washing our car to cutting the lawn to preparing dinner we experience its basic subtle influence that tells us, "you're on the right track."

Because the multitude of tiny successes have become commonplace, we dismiss the value of achieving them, but there is no order of difficulty in successful living, every success whether large or small uses the same basic principles.

These basic principles have been outlined in every major spiritual belief, revealed in the ancient philosophies of enlightened thinking and have appeared on the pages of thousands of books on the Psychology of Self Help. Each speaks to different ears, different belief systems and different cultural inclinations. Nevertheless, all carry the same basic thread.

The Millionaire Maker, has simplified these basic principles for successful living and validated them through the life of a man who used them, lived them and in his own unique way, taught them to millions of people achieving for himself in the process, success on an enormous scale.

His name was Mark Hughes. His life was a model of the basic principles for successful living repeated over and over and over again. Just as the world entered this new century and while still in his mid forties, Mark Hughes passed from this world having climbed mountains most people only see on the postcards of wishful thinking. As you will experience in the pages of this book, Mark Hughes was no different than any of us, what he achieved, all can achieve and more.

Mark Hughes learned the basic laws or principles for successful living. From these he found his life purpose and went on to live it with the passion that accompanies all true purpose. With focused attention on that purpose, he made his dreams come true.

It follows each person will have found the key to their own freedom once they learn and apply the basic laws or principles under which the universe operates. These laws work for beggar and King alike.

Universal mind, also referred to as the Unified Field, Universal Subconscious, God and many other names, is totally neutral. Once It's basic laws are learned and applied to one's life, life bows in humble obedience to our slightest command. It matters not what state of affairs our life was in before our eyes were open, joyful, abundant living will be given to us when these simple laws are learned.

Perhaps the greatest block to the belief that these laws will change our life and allow us to live as the free spirits we were meant to be, is in their basic simplicity. That is the reason why when the world provides us with an archetype that is larger than life, we tend to accept and believe these wonderful changes can also occur in our life.

The Millionaire Maker is such an archetype. It is grand in proportion to worldly attainment and profound in its example of how spirit can be ignited in the hearts and minds of millions of people when one man's passion for a dream is focused on the universal laws for successful living.

> *"The universe is governed by immutable laws. Humanities bondage must be as a result of its ignorance of these laws"*
> **Ernest Holmes - Science of Mind**

The Millionaire Maker portrays a world that is fun, simple and magical. We live in a world, which is largely ignorant of universal laws; the result is a deep-seated fear that we are victims of circumstance. Nothing could be further from the truth!

The possibility for harmony, abundance, peace of mind is within our grasp because it is completely within the grasp of our thoughts. If there is anything in our life that we do not like, we need only **change our mind** to see the changes in our world. These changes in thought produce similar changes in our character, circumstances, relationships and experiences.

Creation, like a diamond has many facets.

The Millionaire Maker gives these facets names such as:

Vision, Integrity, Compassion,
Creativity, Simplicity and Humor.

Each of these facets is an aspect of the living power within us to change our world. Each facet is a **powerful concept** for successful living.

In each chapter these are examined. They are then applied to the life of Mark Hughes as they relate to the incredible success he achieved in pursuing his dream.

By applying these **universal laws** for successful living to your life untold wealth, health and joy will become yours.

*"We are co-creators with God, not puppets on a string
waiting for something to happen"*
Leo Booth

PASSION

"Wheresoever you go, go with all your heart."
Confucius

Mark's dream was fueled by passion. He had a fire in the belly, but far more than that, he absolutely loved every moment of living his dream. Singing his own true song impassioned Mark to heights that few have reached. For Mark, this was a reality he believed all could achieve.

We are Born with a Purpose

What is Your Passion? "Follow Your Bliss"
Joseph Campbell

Living life without a dream is like wasted years spinning our wheels. To experience a successful life of joy we must find that purpose, for that is where we will find our passion. Passion flows effortlessly, unfettered by the "have to's" and the **"need to's"** of careers which conflict with and draw our attention away from our true, life purpose. Passion generates its own magnetism attracting the so-called lucky breaks or synchronistic events that propel dreams forward at lightening speed.

Passion is like a Magnet Creative imagination feeds on passion and brings forth as many ideas as we can absorb. It draws to us exactly the right combination of circumstances, places, things and people we need to fulfill the constantly expanding vision of our dreams. It energizes our body, mind and spirit and improves our immune systems, and it expands our sense of generosity. We feel vitally alive, and overflowing with abundance in every area of our life as it induces us to become acutely aware of the gifts life has to offer, both great and small.

When you like your work, every day is a holiday"
Frank Tyger

Passion is the valve, which allows the floodgates of our highest potential to open and illuminate our spirit so that we may shine our light as an ideal or model for all to share. It lifts, inspires and heals life everywhere. Even the most closed minded person experiences its glow and needs no reason for its existence. He will follow its essence in blind deference to his habitual patterns of pessimism and lack, knowing on some deep level that something new and wonderful is about to emerge. There is an inner knowing that his life is about to change for the better.

This new found light is the catalyst for discovering our passion. As we find an ideal that instills hope in us we can be certain it has impacted that part of us that knows our true, life purpose. This is not an ephemeral impulse that is destined to go down in flames like the moth at the candle. Rather it is the groove in which our unique wheel will roll through effortlessly like rainwater down a mountainside. It will find its own level and nourish the passionate dreams that emanate from it.

We need only remind ourselves that the ideal must not be allowed to degenerate into an idol and in so doing, take away our power. We must **focus our attention** on the higher intention of the ideal and draw its life giving force from within us. Only then do we add our own unique expression to the beautiful tapestry of creation.

"He was in love with his work, and he felt the enthusiasm for it which nothing, but the work we can do well, inspires in us"
William Dean Howells

There is a powerful momentum that grows through passion. It gathers more power unto itself as it proceeds. The little light is drawn to the attraction of the greater light. Both are then magnified. A burning desire also promotes momentum.

However, the intention of a burning desire is oriented to the ego or little self. It is not focused on the highest intention of love, which is geared always toward world service. Therefore it will eventually burn itself out since it does not resonate with the essence of wholeness in which the basic unified oneness of mankind lives.

Nevertheless it is effective and does produce the results we desire on the short term.

Passion on the other hand serves everyone. It is driven by a burning desire guided by love. It inspires the discovery of purpose in everyone it touches and energizes that purpose with increased passion.

A Burning Desire
Guided by Love

"The roads are different, the goal one. When people come (to their purpose) there, all quarrels or differences or disputes that happened along the road are resolved, all hearts are in unison"
J. Rumi

Before I understood the universal laws

I joined Herbalife, in September of 1983, 45 months after its inception in February of 1980. In its brief history the company had grown from the trunk of Mark's Hughes' car in his California neighborhood to all of the United States, Canada and Australia.

At the time Herbalife was generating $15 million per month in sales. In a little over a year that figure would balloon to $90 million per month. And soon, both Mark Hughes and his fledgling company would come under one of the most scathing attacks in the history of the weight loss industry.

I was 37 years old when I joined Herbalife and had been an entrepreneur for almost 17 years before that. During those years I was usually broke and struggling to get some kind of business deal off the ground. Three years before I started my life-changing career with this incredible young company, I founded a company of my own in the Toronto Theater district.

I remember the excitement I had in the early days of building my business. I had little money and no experience in the industry, but I was driven by a burning desire. I saw the incredible potential for my new company in a city third only to

London and New York in the number of live theaters and in the area of audience appeal.

My desire often kept me working 14 hours days and my burning desire to succeed soon drew to me situations and people that assisted me with my plans. In no time I was introduced to a man who offered me a 9,000 square foot office building fully equipped and furnished for free…that's an entire story in itself. Soon I met key individuals who became financial partners in my company including a talented sales manager and a well-known publicity agent. My desire had become contagious.

Within six months I had appeared on several radio and television shows, had the endorsement of the Mayors office and the Arts Council and had been written up in full-page editorials in the three major Toronto newspapers. My advertising budget was a quarter of a million dollars, also through partnership deals. I was in the flow of creative power.

A year later the company folded and I was $100,000 in debt and burned out physically and emotionally. What happened?

Burning Desire versus Passion

I sum it up in three words - LACK OF PASSION. I had a burning desire to create a business, and miraculous things occurred allowing me to establish a foundation for the company, seemingly out of thin air. But, I was not in love with the business or the industry. I saw it as a way to get rich.

We describe passion as a *burning desire guided by love*. There is a gapping hole in what we try to create without love. History has recorded mammoth success stories born of a burning desire only to find the progenitor of the feast starving in spirit, often dying in poverty and obscurity.

Passion, however is what fueled Mark's dream. He had a fire in the belly. He had a song to sing, as do many great innovators. But far more than that, he absolutely loved every moment of living his dream. He didn't merely pursue it - he became it.

"Nothing great in the world has been accomplished without passion"
George Hegel

Living the Dream

Mark Hughes and Herbalife were one. It was difficult to tell where one began and the other ended. Mark would frequently tell his inner circle of top distributors;

"I'm in one business and one business only...Herbalife. Nothin, absolutely nothing distracts me from it."

When the company came under fire in the mid 1980's and experienced a dramatic downturn, Mark brought out his personal check book and made certain everyone got paid. Never was there a delay or a missed paycheck. He kept the company alive knowing in his heart that integrity was the hallmark of his struggling company, and that his distributors needed to feel secure if they were going to stay onboard during those uncertain times.

"First and foremost, I am a distributor. After that I am the Founder, President and CEO of Herbalife."

No Matter What

This **no matter what** attitude was one of the most significant aspects of Mark's teachings. It was a cornerstone that helped shape the company and provided a solid foundation for its distributors. Many that stayed with Herbalife during those dark days now enjoy large five figure incomes **each month**, and are teaching thousands more how to do the same thing based on the legacy Mark left behind.

"Concentrate your energies, your thoughts, and your capital...The wise man puts all his eggs in one basket and watches the basket"
Andrew Carnegie

Mark saved everything from his roots in Herbalife and periodically showed enraptured audiences of tens of thousands of distributors **his personal hand written goals** from the day he started the company.

Really Big Thinking

I remember the first time I saw his journals; I was literally blown away by the enormity of this man's thinking. He had challenged himself *to buy a house each and every month*.

This early appetite for the acquisition of real estate, using his growing fortune, made him a savvy investor. As a result incredible opportunities came his way, as they often do for people who can provide instant solutions when others are in distress.

Through his personal goals he created a financial fortress around his dream so that when he was challenged with an opportunity to expand Herbalife or by an unexpected threat to his dream, he could immediately respond in a tangible and positive way.

Summary

Everyone is born with a special purpose

1-   finding our life purpose inspires a burning desire within us to attain it

2-   allowing the service of others to be our primary objective in attaining our life purpose guides our burning desire by love and converts it into passion

How to Find Your Life Purpose

YOUR PASSION

"Our passions are ourselves"
Anatole France

We have found in our workshops that most people are stumped when they are asked the open-ended question:

"What would you do if you could do anything?"

Most people make a short list of unfulfilled desires then they go blank. The list usually consists of material things, relationships and travel to far away places - perhaps more often related to escape than to an adventurous and joyous life.

Not This - Not That A highly effective concept we have found in our workshops to discover where a person's life purpose and passion lies is in the "not this - not that" technique. This method involves firstly; making a list of everything *we do not want* in our lives, leaving no stone unturned. The old car, the depressing apartment, the dictatorial boss, the dead-end job, the hollow relationships, the over weight body, the crooked teeth, and on and on. This list is usually very easy to create and often somewhat lengthy.

Create a Positive Alternative Affirmation The next step is a little more challenging. It involves creating a statement which is *completely positive and opposite* to each item on our first list. Here is an example from list one and list two.

List #1 - "I hate being in debt!"

List #2 - "I live now financially free and I am thrilled with the life of abundance it affords me. The date is_____."

Note: *A more detailed list of specific steps for creating Positive Affirmations can be found in the special section later in this book entitled:* "Creating Life Changing Affirmations"

Speak as if your Desire has Already Happened Although the date for the acquisition of the desire is in the future, the affirmation is read *as if it were a present date*. The subconscious mind is neutral and does not know anything about time other than what we tell it. If we speak of a future date as if it were now, it sets to work immediately to magnetize that condition into our reality.

Say Exactly What you Want - Nothing Else Another very important point is to frame the affirmation in strictly positive terms. If the condition we do not want is mentioned, *even in positive terms*, we are acknowledging the existence of the condition, stirring up the negative emotions associated with it and empowering it.

For example: "I am now out of debt...." This recognizes that there is a condition known as debt and this will agitate your mind with all the thoughts associated with that condition. We want to draw to ourselves only the conditions and emotions connected to the condition we desire. This is not denial; it is positive creativity and will bring the results we desire effortlessly. Every word is vitally important.

Over-Write Old Negative Programs Universal mind delivers to us exactly what we ask of it. Right now we can hear you protesting that you have asked and asked and asked and many times, perhaps most times, you did not receive what you asked for. It may sound unbelievable, but you DID receive exactly what you asked for.

Beneath the surface of our conscious dialogue is a recording studio playing back soundless messages of old programs we have long forgotten or perhaps did not even realize were there. The dialogue from these programs gets mixed in with our desires and often neutralizes them or even sends messages to universal mind that are opposite to what we thought we wanted and asked for.

On this soundless, invisible level we still believe the messages contained within the programs. Until we erase or over-write these programs, they will cause static and our desires will be delivered with flaws or will not be delivered to us at all.

"God doesn't play dice with universal mind."
Einstein

We eliminate these programs much the same way we do many computer programs, *we write over* them with a new message. That is why it is necessary to be very careful that we say exactly what it is we want to manifest because the new message becomes the new soundless, invisible program. As you can imagine, once you have created it, it works for you without any conscious effort on your part.

Persist This process takes frequent repetition of your new corrective, positive desires because the old programs are often deeply ingrained into the hard drive of our subconscious mind. This is the stage where our life purpose begins to emerge. There will be similarities in the concepts that are the most inspiring and you will feel stimulated when you think about them.

Once the subconscious mind begins to become clear of negative debris, you will soon discover many things floating to the top of your conscious mind that excite you... these are the clues that will lead you to your true heart's desire, your true life purpose.

Your Purpose Will Be Revealed It may come in bits and pieces or as an instantaneous flash, insight or AHA, but *it will come*. And as we said, when you find your life purpose, you will also have found your passion to create it.

Wellness

"Health is not a condition of matter, but of mind"
Mary Baker Eddy

Mark Hughes always looked the picture of dynamic health no matter what situation in which you might find him. He saw life the way he wanted it to be and the universe complied.

The Wellness Revolution

"They go from strength to strength"
Psalm: 84:7

The Wellness Revolution Paul Zane Pilzer - world-renowned economist, presidential advisor and college professor, recently coined a phrase he refers to as: *The Wellness Revolution.* He sees this already $200 billion-dollar industry, reaching one trillion dollars in the next ten years. He claims *"the wellness industry* is on the verge of changing our lives as much as the automobile and personal computer industries did."

A significant motivating factor in this emerging phenomena is the maturing Baby Boomers, now rapidly moving into their 50's. This tidal wave of consumers has swept such industries as baby food, toys, real estate and financial planning into the stratosphere of economic growth and prosperity. Wellness is the top of this rising tide.

The Sickness Industry Wellness should not be confused with health care which is often referred to as the sickness industry and deals with health from a sickness perspective. Wellness products and services primarily focus on healthy people with the objective of preventative methods for making them feel even healthier and look better, while at the same time slowing the effects of aging and preventing disease from developing.

This budding industry embodies a multitude of products and services, some of which include: meditation techniques, affirmations, herbal treatments, holistic body techniques, vitamins, nutritional supplements, health food restaurants, fitness clubs, preventative modalities, medical savings accounts, cosmetic dermatology and weight loss products, to name only a few.

---

*"To keep the body in good health is a duty, for otherwise
we shall not be able to trim the lamp of wisdom"*
Buddha

Baby Boomers Fuel the Growth The prevailing logic of this new phenomena is attractive to the relatively youthful state of millions of people about to retire. These so-called boomers can look forward to many more years of active leisure than their forefathers who traditionally retired at age 65 and lived a comparatively passive life. They basically *grazed* into their golden years. These additional years added to the baby boomers new perspective of relatively energetic activity, present another challenge - the need for far greater capital reserves than previous retiring generations.

It is a wonderful, timely and happy synchronicity that the very industry that is allowing this generation to enjoy many more health filled years of vital living after retirement also offers enormous opportunities for new careers within its own boundaries. Combine this with the incredible growth of *work-from home* business tools now available and you have the ingredients for even greater personal fulfillment in the golden years than ever before.

Few retirees in past generations have expressed self-initiated creativity. As a result, their joy for life was sapped, leading them to live a sedentary lifestyle. However, now there are many ways to express their personal creativity. Combine this with the freedom to chose their work environment, hours and activities and the joy that comes from this freedom to express themselves honestly has the potential to expand their possibilities exponentially.

"The first wealth is health"
Emerson

This 'joy quotient' has many fringe benefits including: more energy, clearer thinking and a more youthful appearance, which all add up to increased immune efficiency. Even the orthodox allopathic medical community openly endorses the value of a *happy lifestyle* for improving one's internal capacity to prevent or reduce disease, and they back it up with innumerable scientific studies.

This is not to suggest that the wellness industry will benefit only those born in the window of time referred to as baby boomers. All of us will come under the beneficent influence of this swiftly changing paradigm, and all of us may capitalize on the opportunities to share these products and services with people all around the world - if we wish from the comfort of our homes.

In a world with many man made challenges to our *joie de vive*, it is a great comfort and a real source of inspiration to feel that there is a new vista opening before us that promises to lift our spirits in many ways, while bridging differences through common and positive objectives.

Health is a State of Being Health is a state of *well being or wholeness*. The dictionary defines wholeness as: *unity or oneness* suggesting that there is - nothing else - it just is. The presence of disease, on any level, therefore suggests that there is in fact something else, That *something else*, does not belong.

"I have put duality away,
I have seen that the two worlds are one"
J. Rumi

In dealing only with health on the level of the body for just a moment, we find that the body in and of itself does not think. When we 'shuffle off the mortal coil', as Shakespeare calls our physical life, it quickly returns to the basic constituents from which it was formed. Without the energizing, animating and coordinating force flowing through it, disintegration is inevitable.

Wholeness is Health The blueprint for wholeness exists within that force or spirit which flows through our mind to the cells of the brain and thence to the trillions of cells in the body. Unless something interferes with the direction of the blueprint, wholeness of the body is the natural and happy result. This includes the world we live in.

It is not specifically the food and nutrients we consume, the hygiene we practice, the exercise we experience, nor the invasive organisms we are exposed to that interfere with a state of wholeness. These are merely channels leading to physical health or potential disease.

Yet even in the presence of physical self-abuse, results are not consistent. We have all seen and heard about people who have lived lives of total self indulgence without sickness, dying well into old age. We have also heard incredible stories of athletes in their prime who suddenly dies on the playing field or court.

Examples like these fly in the face of logic, reason and medical science. How can this be, we wonder. The answer lies in consciously going with the flow, or in most cases, resisting the flow of the blueprint for wholeness. So how do we go with the flow of the blueprint and experience perfect health?

Inner Guidance There is, within all of us, a sense of direction we may refer to as inner guidance. It speaks softly, but without interruption. In the cacophony of our modern lives, hearing this guidance is rare. It does, however come to us clearly in times of urgency, such as when a loved one is in danger, other times when our mind is distracted momentarily perhaps by a sudden noise but especially in quite moments of reflection or meditation.

Most commonly we refer to these moments as coincidental events, hunches, insights or flashes of intuition, always correct in hindsight. Although rare for most people, they are a completely normal aspect of wholeness. In fact, once we recognize the presence of this inner guidance and focus on it, we begin to hear this perfect direction more and more frequently.

"Moments of true consciousness, unconditioned by the self, are usually fleeting but indelible"
Anne Bancroft

When this begins to occur, the right foods and nutrients, the correct exercise, the exact quality and quantity of personal care we ourselves require for perfect health will be shown to us. Further, our internal immune response system will function at optimum levels blocking anything, which is not in harmony with our perfect state of wholeness or well being.

He Saw the Future

"He who has health has hope,
and he who has hope has everything"
Arabian Proverb

A Visionary Mark Hughes saw the personal needs in all he met and in many ways he helped fill those needs better than anyone else in his era. He innately understood timing as well as a woman awaiting the birth of her newborn child knows the exact moment her child will be born.

This is timing connected with an inner wisdom. Mark was a visionary that saw a unique opportunity to introduce the ancient science of natural herbal nutrition into the emotional area of weight loss, just at a moment in history when interest in nutrition began skyrocketing in the western world.

This was a stroke of genius. Whether by default or by intention, Mark constantly listened to the coaching of his inner guide. It is likely, in his humble way he simply attributed this habit as the natural inclination to follow frequent hunches.

He also knew that western psychology was highly entrepreneurial. Combining the innovation of herbal nutrition with weight loss, while offering these products to the public through a marketing system that allowed people to work part time or full time, from home, and get paid in direct proportion to the value they brought to the marketplace, was also perfect timing.

"World progress needs entrepreneurs"
Sir John Templeton

Mark knew that the evolution of home-based businesses was about to explode, in fact he was one of the pioneers in its evolution. He had experienced this newly developing concept first hand in two separate companies a few years before he founded Herbalife.

In his apprenticeship he became the number one distributor in record time in both companies. In creating "Herbalife" Mark saw that his new company could reach the maximum number of people in the shortest time by employing the same *home-based marketing principle* he had been successful with before.

Add to this, the fact that each home-based distributor became emotionally involved with the products as customers first and as distributors second, and the winning formula was complete. It needed only to be shared in the proper way with the world and the world would beat a path to his doorstep.

As you will experience throughout this book, this involved the powerful Keys, which he modeled for everyone in his company through his personal character and life.

Perhaps the most poignant of these traits was Mark's personal dedication to an attitude of wellness which he consistently displayed. Mark wore a huge smile and was filled with joy; he always looked the picture of dynamic health. No matter what situation in which you might find him, his dress matched his physical appearance. Even when dressed casually, he never looked less than impeccable and that was the consistent image of the company, which he headed.

It could certainly be said that his life was not perfect, however if anyone wishes to employ the fallible practice of judging another, we need look no further than his stupendous and heroic accomplishments to witness what Mark Hughes was constantly creating on the internal screen of his consciousness.

"Work is love made visible"
Kahil Gibran

He saw life the way he wanted to live it and Universal Mind responded with, *your wish is my command.* This is how it works for all of us. When we are clear about what it is we want to bring forth and we affirm it through dedicated focus, Universal Mind will comply by giving us that which we desire. Mark's intentions and focused dreams for Herbalife were crystal clear and what occurred matched what he dreamt about. In this way he set the mold and the pace that millions of people now emulate around the world.

Today, because of Mark Hughes' dedication to making his dream a reality, millions of people around the world have access to good, sound; basic nutrition based on the science of herbs. And many more people are benefiting in a financially, while living the life of the rich and famous. Of far more importance, they are teaching others what they have learned through the growth of their character, from this masterful dream-maker Mark Hughes.

It is in this area of personal growth that an enormous ripple effect is now occurring which is touching the entire world. The world is and will continue to see the miraculous effects of Mark's incredible vision and the tidal wave of his dream that came true will live on and on.

"You shall know them by their fruits"
Matthew 7:16

Going Within

"A vision sets direction for thinking and action"
Edward de Bono

What Could Be Great loss often forces a person to withdraw inside himself. The loss may be so deep that an immense emptiness is left where a person, place or thing once lived. In this dark void, it is possible to become aware of a part of himself he did not know existed.

Many people are inspired to reach for a higher power. Some find God during these difficult times, most find a higher meaning or purpose to their life. As a result, during this period of self-discovery it is possible to receive life-changing insights, which lead to major life decisions.

Those that seek a higher perspective find themselves on new ground and in this new state of consciousness, miracles begin to occur as they find synchronistic moments are everyday happenings. *What has been,* is replaced by *what could be.* This is the territory where infinite possibilities await. It's a place *where dreams really do come true.*

The Universal Plan The direction that precedes the experience of connecting with a higher perspective often comes from an awareness of a vision or partial vision of the universal plan. There is a sense or a knowing that ultimately, everything is going to turn out right, that they will be guided to that portion of the universal plan that is their true life purpose.

The sheer grandeur of the event is both deeply personal while at the same moment, all encompassing as the recipient realizes in order for her to fulfill her true life purpose, whether grand or modest, she must share with the world the gift she has been given. She must in some way, through her personal life purpose, add to the stairs leading mankind home.

Vision Arrives Spontaneously True vision arrives spontaneously and cannot be forced or manipulated into blessing us with its gifts of purpose and passion. As with the genuine creative genius these moments of discovery must be allowed to come forth with gentle receptivity. Clutching and clawing tenses and closes the portal to this heightened awareness.

True vision never arrives for those who seek to limit the creative expression of mankind in any way. The higher aspirations of the inner spirit always tend toward service, uniting and wholeness.

It is through those doors that *our better angels* or higher thoughts *ascend and descend.* Vision cannot be appropriated with the physical eyes but through the single eye through which the whole body of mankind shall one day be full of light or in a state of enlightened self-awareness.

Cultivating our Receptivity Until recently, most people have distracted from their inner guide and lived artificially. Their focus has been on the thought-programs of past experience or on the future - both near and far. Initially this new habit of focusing attention inward may feel uncomfortable.

As a society, people have been in the habit of listening to direction that comes from sources with big names and impressive titles. However, the credibility of these sources has now become intolerably suspect and there is a desperate cry for guidance that is reliable and truthful.

Cultivating our receptivity for True vision is accomplished through the practice of redirecting our focus inward to the True source of all we consciously experience with our physical senses outside. In this way we place no false idols or gods between our true-life purpose and us.

"Vision looks inward and becomes duty. Vision looks outward and becomes aspiration. Vision looks upward and becomes faith.
Stephen S. Wise

Collectively, we have arrived at a moment in the evolution of mankind when we are ready to accept the possibility that infallible guidance can be received by each of us by going within.

A Dream is Born
Passion is Awakened

"Only he who can see the invisible can do the impossible"
Frank Gaines

Roots One tiny historical reference is essential to open the book of dreams Mark lived within. It is particularly auspicious while tragic that the passing of Mark's mother should inspire the birth of heroic change.

As the story goes, Marks' mother, an actress and single parent, struggled for years with her weight. It seems inconceivable that thirty pounds could be so significant a challenge that it could one day claim her life. However the movie industry can be seen as ruthless to a beautiful young woman who naturally wished to use every attribute she had to break into the world of her dreams.

She tried every weight loss diet available at the time and finally succumbed to a lethal cocktail of amphetamines and prescription sleeping pills which helped her come down from the *speed* high she experienced on the so-called powerful weight loss drug.

She became hooked on the combination of dangerous drugs and increased her habit by visiting several doctors at the same time. Eventually, she became the all too common victim of an overdose at the tender age of thirty-six.

The heart broken teenager's experience became a hole in his spirit that would soon be filled by the staff and banner of Herbalife.

Before that day however, Mark would quickly rise to the pinnacle of success in two separate ill fated weight loss companies that soon pulled the rug out from under him through poor management and lack of integrity. Once again, his heartbreak became his inspiration. Already, at twenty one, the young millionaire-maker was learning the incredible boomerang power of using adversity to fuel dreams

During his brief foray into the weight loss industry, Mark befriended Dr. Richard (Dick) Marconi who saw the passion for power growing within him.

Dr. Marconi was a well established manufacturer in the vitamin industry and offered Mark an opportunity to meet with various members of the Chinese Trade delegation who were introducing the 3,000 year old science of Chinese herbal medicine to the west. Little did anyone realize at the time that Mark would become the champion of the science of herbal medicine to the world.

The impressionable young Mark Hughes was literally blown away by the established reputation herbs had to stimulate the natural healing ability of the body. It was at this point that he experienced what might be called a giant AHA, which would soon become the impetus to bring forth the vision he had for changing the world.

Even in the early years I remember this tall, long haired kid ending his inspirational training seminars with an ecstatic cry: *We're gonna CHANGE the nutritional habits of the entire world with these incredible products.*" The audience never failed to go wild, riding the wave of Mark's passion. His concept was simple, if not revolutionary. He knew that millions of people would do just about anything to lose a few pounds.

""A wounded deer leaps the highest"
Emily Dickinson

Firstly, his experience with his mother, then his belated meteoric rise to fame in the weight loss industry had proven that fact to him. In Mark's unique way he used to tell us about his original idea:

"What if we SNUCK herbs in ta nutritional weight loss products, people will start to lose weight AND feel great…they'll ask us, 'how come?' Then we got a chance to explain WHY they're feelin better and keep em on the products fer life."

Then he'd grin from ear to ear and laugh out loud, and everyone would break into uproarious laughter. Mark's joy for living was contagious and in all the years I knew him, he continued to exhibit the gleeful joy of a child about the dream he was living and sharing with millions of people.

The product vision was truly simple yet revolutionary by any western standard in health care at the time. It worked this way:

First, the body received good sound basic nutrition in balance every day through the use of quality nutritional products and recommended balanced eating. Then, due to the cleansing and healing effect of herbs on the body's absorption system, all the nutrition consumed becomes available to the cells of the body. This gives the body the best chance of improving or healing itself of stresses or dis-eases and receiving excellent health, vitality, energy and a feeling of well being.

It only stood to reason that as a result of feeling better many customers would consider remaining on the products after they lost the weight they wanted to. This also improved the chances they would maintain their ideal weight, the most significant challenge dieters experience after succeeding on a diet.

With this unique vision and with the help of Dr. Marconi, on a *shoestring* budget, Mark Hughes founded Herbalife on February 1st, 1980. He began grandly with a Beverly Hills address.

As Mark put it: *"90% of Beverly Hills is rich and beautiful, "10% is ugly. That's where we were, but we had the fancy address we could use when we invited people to look at the opportunity. I invited fifteen of my best friends down and told them we were going to change the nutritional habits of the world with this incredible product. At that point I pulled out a baggy full of powder." He'd laugh. "Which in Los Angeles in the 80's was a dangerous thing to do. My friends thought I was crazy and told me I was nuts."*

"The only ones among you who will be really happy are those who will have sought and found how to serve"
Albert Schweitzer

In the first few days of business the resolute young man began selling his unique, life-changing products from the trunk of his car. He loved sharing the story of this first less-than-business-opportunity-meeting. And always, he'd break out laughing like a little kid, even twenty years after the first time he told the story.

Mark quickly recovered from the sting of his friend's initial rejection, and went on to explain how he got his first few customers. *"My granny's incredible. You gotta meet her. She's got ratchet mouth, she'll talk to anybody!"* Then he would make a clever little gesture with his hands to show how a ratchet mouth opened and closed.

"My granny got on these incredible products and was so excited when she lost the weight she wanted to, she told everyone down at the beauty parlor and first thing ya know. I had my first 16 customers."

He'd tell these kinds of stories with absolute joy. Everyone loved his intimate sharing and melted in its warmth.

From this humble beginning Mark then recruited his first *teachable* distributor, Geri Cvitanovich. Geri was a shy part time school teacher and grocery checker. He said: *"Geri, I want you to call up your mother and ask her to please help you to get your business started by becoming your first customer."*

Despite her initial anxiousness, Mark was right by her side and through his loving, enthusiastic encouragement she decided to make the call. Much to Geri's total surprise, her mother said yes and Geri never looked back.

Today she has become an icon of THE HUGHES LEGACY how *simple* the spirit of Mark's dream can be used to draw greatness from the jaws of mediocrity. She now lives in an ocean-side mansion in Hawaii and travels the world sharing Mark's simple instructions for success with thousands of eager distributors, with the same loving passion Mark used to inspire her.

Stick to Your Dream

"The ultimate measure of a man is not where he stands in moments of comfort and convenience, but where he stands at times of challenge and controversy"
Dr. Martin Luther King Jr

So You Have Found Your Life's Purpose So you have found your life purpose and your entire being is aflame with the passion to live and achieve it. You have seeded your field, lovingly nurtured it and young healthy growth can be seen far and wide. And now the multitudes are beginning to gather around your crops to partake of the feast.

Meanwhile, scouts have been sent out from nearby ancient fields to find out what all the fuss is about. In the beginning, your humble efforts are seen as childish and unworthy of their attention. *"The crows will eat their puny harvest."* They proclaim.

Later, when the tender shoots of your initial endeavors poke their eager heads through the soil, the ancient farmers look down from their ivory towers in mock praise, tolerant but mildly irritated by the little thorn that would dare threaten to pierce their sides.

But then the day comes when the banner of your dream is held high, your harvest has become rich and the multitudes have beaten a path to your door. What do they say? They cannot complain their goods are rotting on shelves while the more delectable fruit of your harvest is sought out.

Destroy the Dream *"Sour grapes!"* Would be the crowd's reply. No! They would plot a less obvious demise of your dream. *"We must discredit this upstart. We must put him in his place once and for all. Let us gather our forces from far and wide, the visible and especially the hidden. Let us crush* *this vermin before his fresh ideas encroach upon our ancient garden and the hapless rabble discover our time has past."*

And so the battle cry begins. The media heralds the discovery of an outrageous fraud. Politicians, eager to feather nests with a controversial issue, join the witch-hunt. The pay-offs are put in place and the mud begins to fly.

How shines the brilliance of your sun now? Can your passion remain ablaze while your detractors pour their scurrilous venom upon your dreams? Can you withstand the false prophets of doom who proclaim your lack of character? Can you fight the good fight, holding to the pure essence that underpins your life purpose?

Burn Your Bridges It is a *no matter what,* attitude. It is a decision to follow through with your dreams knowing that long ago you burned your bridges and you can never go back to what once was. The only direction you can go is forward. Further, it is an unshakable conviction in the depths of your soul that you know what you have dreamed is right and true and part of a much grander dream than the world or you have yet to learn.

It is the decision, as **Rudyard Kipling** said:

"to risk it all on a game of pitch and toss"...

To risk it all on a game of pitch and toss, undisturbed by what end may come of the contest. Because you know, even if you should lose this battle, in the end you will win the *internal* war.

And if you should fall, pick yourself back up, re-trench, stand tall, take a deep breath and set out again and again and again on the road from which you can never retreat, the road of your passion, your purpose, your destiny, your dream, staying focused until at last it stands in all its brilliance before you.

The Integrity to Keep
His Dream Alive

"All Good will be Attacked"
Jim Rohn

Success is Challenged Before the age when most people graduate College, Mark Hughes had achieved worldly success on a scale few have ever dreamed about let alone reached for - and attained. In all probability only a handful of people in history have reached this level of success which in turn created vast opportunities to change lives for so many people in so many ways.

Certainly timing is a critical factor in attaining this echelon of success. In the late 1970's and early 1980's the mindset of being *upwardly mobile* was rampant. The age of yuppies had arrived and appearance, health and fitness were an integral part of this mainstream thinking as work-a-holics were fueling the dash for cash and status.

Nevertheless, it would take much more than good timing. Mark would need to hold fast to his vision if Herbalife was to survive the dark cloud that was to accompany his early success.

What more logical place for a nutritional weight loss company to put down roots than in Beverly Hills, California. Mark's previous experience in the industry, while brief, had been hugely successful despite his eventual losses with the companies he worked with.

Even so, we believe it was the bitter disappointments in Mark's life more than his successes that fueled his passion to live and achieve his dreams. By the mid 1980's Herbalife

49

had reached a benchmark few corporations had ever achieved, over $90 million a month in sales.

Extrapolated, that's over $1 billion a year, a feat Herbalife was certain to attain in its sixth year in business had Mark's biggest challenge to date not occurred.

"Opposition inflames the enthusiast, it never converts him"
J.C.F. von Schiller

A few months later it seemed the entire world had joined forces against both Herbalife and Mark Hughes personally. He was now in his mid twenties and had created a personal fortune few people could even imagine. When the world he sought to help, launched a soul crushing attack on his company and his personal integrity, he could have simply retired. BUT HE HUNG IN!

Instead of falling back into the comfort of his wealth, he risked it all and stood tall. What followed would make seasoned executives' heads spin. But Mark was not in this class of executive, he was a young passionate entrepreneur who loved people and believed in his dream. Like the Jimmy Stewart character in "Mr. Smith goes to Washington", he was *unaware* that he could not beat the vested interests of corporate America.

Mark might have been personally wounded but he didn't appear to be affected by the scathing newspaper reports that said, "Herbalife products kill people," adding attacks on him personally, questioning his ability and credentials to run a multimillion dollar company.

The youthful longhaired Mark Hughes countered the attack by staging a march on Washington with a thousand distributors and customers. Shortly afterward he sat before a Senate Sub Committee investigating false claims that were waged against the weight loss industry.

Part of this investigation was played out in front of a live television audience. Mark spoke to the panel of Senators with the confidence that was part of his success. He told them: *"You guys have no business judging my weight loss company when yer all so fat yerselves"*

As you can imagine, that statement didn't sit well with his interrogators. Meanwhile, back in the Herbalife community, many customers and distributors alike were jumping ship. This additional challenge quickly began evaporating the company's income.

"Only those who risk going too far can possible find out how far one can go"
T.S. Elliot

However, Mark did not allow these difficulties to divert him one bit from his dream. He dug into his personal assets and business continued as usual.

The battle lasted almost two years and ended with the government backing away from its charges. A deal was struck and the charges were dropped in return for Herbalife agreeing to pay just under $1 million in legal bills. The media buried this information in tiny newspaper articles. No apologies were forthcoming from the media, the FDA, or the government.

The Tables Turn By the 90's; the Herbalife products had reached and improved the quality of living for millions of people around the world. With that success, Mark's fame grew as the leader of one of the fastest growing companies in natural health and weight management. As a result he began to receive awards for his humanitarian contribution to the world. Many of these awards were given to him from the very same people who had spoken out against him so vehemently in the 80's.

I remember sitting with the President's Team on one occasion when Mark had just received such an award. He named the people who had given him the award, then went on to say that these same *guys* were the ones who had attacked him during the battle ten years earlier. He broke into a wonderful Mark Hughes laugh, his eyes welled up with tears, he got choked and muttered, *"Go Figure."*

Mark's image was projected on a huge screen monitor and his humanity could be clearly seen from every seat in the entire arena. Mark always appeared larger than life in these meetings and it was not unusual to see him shaking his head and weeping after telling a story like the one above. At this particular meeting he received a standing ovation which probably lasted a full ten minutes as Mariah Carey's song *"Hero"* played triumphantly in the background.

"Only by cultivating the virtue of wholeness and by returning injury with kindness can there by true harmony. Therefore one deep virtue is to always give without expecting gratitude"
Lao Tzu

When the audience finally took their seats many of the distributors who had participated in the march on Washington paid homage to Mark with *an Herbalife historical video tribute* to the man that had stood tall and saved his dream when the opposition sought to destroy his company.

Mark's courage and dedication to protect his dream while under fire together with his *no matter what* attitude, set the standard for thousands of Herbalife devotees world wide to pursue their dreams with the same courage and dedication.

No matter what the world or their circumstances might tell them, they had learned through this man's heartfelt intention and enthusiastic actions to stand tall and never stop believing in their dreams.

He could have compromised his dream and sold out, but *he risked ALL to gain ALL.* Many people had encouraged him to defend his integrity but *he never focused on the problem, he always chose the solution.*

When people asked him why he didn't fight to protect his name his answer was a quote from one of his mentors, internationally renowned motivational speaker Jim Rohn: *"Things that do not need to be said, need NOT be said!"*

"No person was ever honored for what they received. Honor has been the reward for what he gave"
Calvin Coolidge

Mark knew that what we resist, persists, what we focus our attention on expands, and that the truth needs no defense, only demonstration. Mark's life was a living representation of integrity, of living his dream every moment and standing unshakably firm in his intent to see it to fruition.

This was most apparent in his passionate desire to share his dream with anyone who wished to change his life for the better, and who was willing to find his own dream and the passion to achieve it.

Summary

Life purpose is the primary focus for existence

1-   all great ideals will be challenged

2-   once our life purpose is found we must develop a "no matter what " attitude toward its achievement

Humility

---

*"I believe the first test of a truly
great man is his humility."*
John Ruskin

It was typical for Mark to highlight his incredible achievements in humble ways. He was a wizard at being a child and bringing the little child in all of us to the surface.

Letting Go

"Real humility is internal and has its origin in wisdom"
Rabbi Nahman of Bratslav

Separation There is a human tendency to create barriers that separate us from what we perceive as different from ourselves. We see this in every walk of life. In those people, places or circumstances that we fear, we separate ourselves through judgment, criticism and attack. In those people, places and circumstances we love, we idolize, worship and hold them up as trophies and vicariously bask in the sunlight of their grandeur.

Both experiences are disillusioning at best because at a deep inner level, separation is a lonely, abnormal practice. In truth, we are all One, sharing a limitless, indivisible power. When we are secure in this knowing and express a sense of oneness with all life, we experience true joy.

Allowing Humility is not weakness; on the contrary it is one of the most powerful tools in the universe because of its quality of *allowing*. Each of us is a facet in the diamond of the Universal Mind, God, or whatever name you feel comfortable with. All of us are created in Its image. This image is not physical; It is pure Spirit, pure Love, pure potential, possessing infinite possibilities. The fact that we do not demonstrate this image is not the fault of the Benefactor of It, but of our lack of awareness of this potential within us.

Through generational amnesia we are ignorant of our Oneness with Universal Mind, and through our free will we have chosen to separate ourselves from the power that resides within ourselves. In this *point of power*, infinite possibilities reside. As a result of our ignorance we have created a world of limitation, conflict and pain.

"Humility opens the door to progress"
Sir John Templeton

However, when we *allow* ourselves to *let go*, and let the wisdom, love and power that is our true essence to flow through us, we begin to experience a world filled with miraculous circumstances, which become the norm in our everyday life.

Will Power Humility is a prerequisite if we want to move the modern day mountains that stand in the way of our dreams coming true. Humbly releasing our little will to the infinite Will of our creator illustrates that we have gained a degree of wisdom. The inner guidance that flows from that fountain of pure knowledge will not only show us the "how to's" we require to create our dreams, It will design and create them for us.

The Course in Miracles states: *"Our little will is like the little sunbeam, that in its colossal arrogance has decided it is the sun, like the drop of water that deems itself to be the ocean."* With this unimaginable pomposity, it is no surprise that fear is so prevalent in our world. To make the fullest demonstration of our highest potential we must humbly allow the floodgates to open and let flow the fount of Universal Mind into our lives and our dreams.

"Being humble does not mean being passive and retiring. It means seeing ourselves clearly in order to act. Humility is the launching pad for aggressive growth."
Marvin Gawryn

Fun and Simple

"He that humbles himself shall be exalted"
Matthew: 23:12

Humble Grandeur On a very basic level Mark Hughes had an innate understanding of the value of humility. He took every opportunity to reduce the influence that his success, good looks, fame, power and money might have on people to separate him from his family of distributors, staff and everyone with whom he had daily interaction.

It was typical for Mark to highlight his incredible achievements in humble ways. An Herbalife event was always a gala event; no expense was spared to create an environment of opulence, fun, and recognition. No one who attended these events could doubt for a moment that indeed, *anything is possible* if a few basic principles are followed.

It was at these grand occasions that Mark would drag out remnants of his humble beginnings as a *millionaire maker*. He'd bend over in laughter, slap his leg several times and follow this up with huge screen photos of the original packaging he used to launch his empire.

"Look at these ugly pages." He would laugh. "Can you believe this was our first career manual for C H A N G I N G the world? It's the worst manual ever created. Its got ink smears, all kinna typos and spelling mistakes everywhere. Who woulda thought we'd be here today with this awful stuff, hunh?"

The crowd would scream and hoot and clap for minutes in ecstatic wonder. There was this image of a handsome, young multi-millionaire dressed impeccably, playing in a giant sandbox. You could *slice the love* in the room like a beautiful wedding cake.

The grandiose was always subdued to allow everyone to see that the *outer thing* was not his primary focus. Every person could feel a sense of *self empowerment* in Mark's presence, realizing that the simple and humble stage-props Mark lovingly made fun of, were not the reasons that Herbalife had become the recognized worldwide leader in weight loss and nutrition.

An invisible spirit or essence was behind the packaging; something Mark helped everyone feel they too possessed. Mark was a wizard at being a child and bringing the little child in all of us to the surface, to run free and express ourselves with reckless abandon. I've seen huge macho men with stony faced glares melt in his presence, perhaps totally unaware of the quantum leap they had just taken in learning how to live life more fully. Mark had a habit of using the word *little* to describe spectacular things.

He'd say:

"Look at this guy on the can of Formula #1. Its a picture of me, little Marky walking hand in hand with the girl friend I was dating. See us walking into the sunset with the mountains in the background. It's supposed to be a happy, healthy looking young couple who takes the products. Oh man, was I corny back then!"

"Subdue pride through humility"
Jainism

Casual or elegant, he always looked rich and immaculate. And more than likely the car he was referring to was a Bentley or a Rolls but he gave you a mental image of a little kid on his first job, wearing a hundred dollar suit off the rack, driving an old beat up Toyota.

Everyone identified with him and could sense his presence, side by side, on the front lines with them, facing their worst fears as they struggled to be the best they could be. If Mark did anything he, *"cleaned up great.."* as he put it, followed always with a huge belly laugh.

He was a picture of magnificent detachment. He carried a personal aura of opulence much as Nieman Marcus, Cartier or The Ritz immediately brings to mind. But he gave it no special importance. Mark knew it was both the right and the inheritance of all of God's children to live abundantly.

I believe the driving motivation for Mark was, *"to be the master of his world, rather than the servant of it."* I remember one occasion when I was chatting with Mark and a few of his staff in an anteroom behind a large convention hall we were using for an all day training. Mark was preparing to go on stage and needed to connect a remote microphone to himself. As usual, he was fastidious about his appearance and did not want wires to show hanging off his suit.

Just before he began preparing, I asked him about the beautiful boots he was wearing that day and Mark casually explained where I could contact his friend in Italy to get some made, as if everyone bought their shoes that way.

"to be in the world but not of it."
John 17:14

At that moment he stood up and began undressing. I looked bug-eyed at his two female assistants across the table who were smiling. He had his back turned to us and had his pants half way down as he fished some of the wires under his shirt so that he could clip the microphone behind his tie.

He turned his head and began laughing in his customary infectious manner and said: *"You guys know me right. No big deal, eh."* I'm Canadian, so he likely added 'eh' as a buzzword to make me feel extra comfortable with the unusual scene. The subtle tension that had begun to rise, dissolved and, as usual, we all broke into belly laughs.

In that wonderful moment Mark revealed himself as the boy-next-door-kind-of guy, temporarily wearing a rented tuxedo for the school prom. It really was no big deal to him. He wore *the appropriate costume* for this particular audience. His objective always remained the same: *to improve the lives of as many people as he could and take his dream around the world.*

Summary

Universal Will fulfils life purpose

1-   our little will can only achieve what it can see; always this involves limitations, no matter how large its dreams may be

2-   allowing our will to be guided by the Will of the Universal Mind instills a limitless attitude toward achievement of our Life Purpose

Recognition

"Recognition is the greatest motivator"
Gerard C. Eakedale

The meetings were one big recognition festival. Mark highlighted every achievement through testimonies.

An Act of Love

"Anything done for another is done for oneself"
Boniface VIII

Recognition Lifts Spirits To give genuine acknowledgment to the accomplishments of others is an act of love. Recognizing another's worth extends a part of us and feeds the entire being of the one on the receiving end.

We are all familiar with the way we feel when we are recognized. Few things lift our spirits, clear our minds and energize our bodies more than being appreciated. So powerful is this inner desire for acknowledgment that years after the passing of parents, many people are still doing things to gain their acceptance, living out their dreams for them, often-times neglecting their own dreams.

People will accept a paycheck well below the value of their service in exchange for a title. The entire fashion, cosmetics and fragrance industries are fueled and guided by people's insatiable need for acceptance. And the advertising industry invests a large portion of their time, energy and resources to understand exactly what will make people feel special and look important in the eyes of their family, friends and peers.

The World Craves Recognition We need not look further than the music and movie industry to see the impact recognition has on we humans. Several award ceremonies occur virtually every month recognizing some aspect of stardom in this dream world. We crave to be loved, needing to know we are important, and that in the scheme of things, somehow we count for something. We will do extraordinary things to obtain a feeling of acceptance.

But, while recognition is an invaluable aspect of the motivation of human potential, it is important to understand there are two different forms of it, one temporary and the other eternal.

Most recognition from the very small to the great is for things *we do* and *things we have done* - both external activities. All that is external is temporary and is usually gone in an instant. One award winner put it this way: *"Your not in the sun long enough to get a tan."* How quickly we forget a famous movie star that has not appeared in a film for a year or two.

The same is true in every walk of life and feels just as disheartening as the emotion of elation felt when recognition came knocking at our door.

Who We Are is More Important This brings us to the second form of recognition, the acknowledgment *of who we really are*. We have all heard about people who achieved great things in life in the eyes of the world only to discover later that they had a closet full of skeletons. Their accomplishments were made at the expense of others.

Less frequently we hear of lofty achievement in the area of personal development accompanied by great works. When these individuals are acknowledged their accomplishments are synonymous with who they truly are.

The person and their accomplishments live eternally together with the quality of spirit they achieved. They are one in the same. Ghandi, Martin Luther King Jr., Mother Teresa, Abraham Lincoln, St. Francis of Assisi, and Jesus immediately inspire a picture of both wondrous works and virtuous spirits.

To the extent a person has attained lofty spiritual growth they are equally *detached from the need for recognition.*

They have reached the level of true attainment where acceptance is eternal, emanating from the highest source.

How will we then recognize true achievement in others? We do this first and foremost by recognizing that we are *spiritual beings having a physical human experience,* and as such most of us still require the ephemeral, temporary stroking that nurtures our sense of self worth.

"The higher the top, the lower the drop."

This is similar to a man with a fractured leg using a crutch to help support him while his limitation heals. In this case the fracture is the belief that we are limited in any way.

As our sense of self-value expands, we turn our attention more and more inward toward the recognition of our true value. Until the day of awakening to our true Self it is normal for us to gratefully accept recognition when it comes without making it a means to an end for our happiness.

False idolatry keeps us looking for acceptance outside ourselves, keeping our *little self*-alive. Wherever possible, we need to acknowledge the greatness that resides within the true Self, both in others and ourselves. Sometimes with trophies, pins and certificates, but also and often with the praise of the soul that seeks the highest within.

There is a word for this in the east, often accompanied by folded hands and a bow:

"Namaste - The spirit of Wholeness within me recognizes the spirit of Wholeness within you"

"Have no false God's before me"
Exodus 20:3

66

Meet - Greet and Recognize

*"The greatest efforts of the race have always
been traceable to the love of praise"*
John Ruskin

Testimonies and Recognition Mark Hughes highlighted every achievement through testimonies. In the early days of Herbalife meetings, called BOM's or Business Opportunity Meetings, were held three times per week in hundreds of cities.

These meetings were simple and included three components: Firstly, a basic history of the company which recognized Mark's mother, Dr. Marconi the manufacturer of the products, the Chinese tradition of herbal medicine and Mark's granny.

Next came an explanation of the products followed by several distributors marching across the front of the room enthusiastically explaining their successful results on the products. Tears often flowed and applause filled the room throughout these testimonies.

Finally, the business opportunity was explained, again followed by distributors marching across the front of the room and emotionally telling the audience about the success they had achieved sharing the products with customers and helping other distributors do the same. Once again tears and applause accompanied the testimonies.

The meetings were one big recognition festival. The concept worked! People joined the company in droves; the company expanded and became one of the fastest growing corporations in the history of America at the time. With the introduction of more effective communication technology many variations of this concept are still in use throughout the world today.

Of all the events in which I saw Mark participate, none brought him greater joy than recognizing the efforts and achievements of his distributors and the customers who used the products.

Achievement Awareness During the early 90's when Herbalife was entering its second giant growth wave, I was part of a new international training concept that involved daylong events in many cities called *"supervisor schools."* These schools were used in conjunction with live and recorded training calls that distributors could tap into via conference calls. In modern training today this is commonplace, however at the time it was unique.

Herbalife was always on the cutting edge of innovative techniques for training and motivating its distributors. I had been doing these schools and conference calls for a few months when I attended an extravaganza at the Universal Theater in Los Angeles. Without prior warning Mark asked all the trainers to come up on stage where we were given a crystal trophy.

The day's schedule was tight, filled with many events, yet Mark came up to me, stopped and put his arm around my shoulder, then whispered in my ear how proud he was of a particular training call I had done a few nights before.

The audience was not aware of what he said, but in that tiny gesture, he showed me far greater recognition than the stage appearance or trophy could have ever done. Nothing more was said and nothing was asked of me, but as the scope and size of the training expanded with the company's phenomenal growth, I always made myself available to fly out to a city for a few days and contribute.

Mark understood that recognition was frequently far more valuable than financial compensation to inspire people to extend themselves into the circle of giving.

"We are all motivated by a keen desire for praise, and the better a person is, the more they are inspired by glory"
Cicero

Recognition Fosters Leadership With the help of *Jim Rohn, Mark created a Leadership Recognition system called the *"Tab Team."* It provided the physical recognition of beautifully designed jeweled pins that designated what level a distributor had achieved and offered a bonus system that helped lift hundreds of people to *the status of millionaire* very soon after attaining this special status. But of far more value was the subtle influence that this recognition had on every member of this growing team.

Immediately after qualifying for *"Tab Team,"* a new sense of responsibility began to seep into the hearts and minds of every member. The seeds of leadership sprouted in fertile ground, nurtured by focused thought and recognition. The result was the acceptance of a greater challenge that sought to serve at loftier levels.

Mark knew that recognition bred leadership on every rung of the ladder of Self-Development and he joyfully poured it out in abundance. As a result, Mark was the one most recognized, and the one who took on more responsibility for the welfare of others. He always raised the bar by his own leadership example.

"We receive freely when we give freely"
Anonymous

Summary

We are spiritual beings having a physical experience

1-   the world we experience is a partial and temporary expression of who and what we are, idolizing anything within it, limits our ability to live successfully

2-   awareness of our oneness with Universal Mind recognizes there is no need for outside approval and allows us to stand confidently on its perfection

Simplicity & Affirmation

"Nothing is more simple than greatness;
indeed, to be simple is to be great"
Ralph Waldo Emerson

Mark Hughes was a master of simplicity. He used his humble beginnings as a banner for all to see that they too could replicate what he had done.

Filling the Mold

"Advance confidently in the direction of your dreams"
Henry David Thoreau

What We Repeat - We Entreat Affirmation is another word for prayer. What we repeat we entreat, petition, request or pray for. The influence repetition has on our lives is beyond all description. It encompasses every aspect of our lives since it calls upon the ineffable power of Universal Mind itself to fill the mold we are creating with our focused thought, thereby bringing it into outward expression in our lives.

We all do this in an almost involuntary way each day through our most frequently expressed mottoes, slogans, clichés and catch phrases. Many of these self-fulfilling prophecies are ingrained into our subconscious minds through the multitude of advertisements we are exposed to each day.

Others are provided through the close associations we form, and many come through the belief systems we adhere to. When we truly understand the power that repetitive statements have on the quality of our lives, we become highly selective about the words that we allow to flow into our thoughts and take root in our subconscious mind.

When we find discomfort in any area of our lives we need not look further than the most frequently repeated ideas that we allow to echo *like rote* through our minds.

"The ills from which we are suffering have had their seat in the very foundation of human thought"
Teilhard de Chardin

The Good News However, that which has been planted in the subconscious mind and patiently cultivated, perhaps for many years, may also be uprooted, thereby changing the program and its effects in our lives. Affirmation is a powerful tool for sculpting the hard drive of our subconscious minds into a beautiful image of what we desire to manifest in our lives.

Wherever we see a dark spot in our lives, a bump in the road, a lack or limitation of any kind, a relationship that needs healing, a condition in our bodies that is less than vital, alive and perfect, we can positively influence these things through a change in the program that is in back of them in our subconscious minds.

Keep Affirmations Simple Affirmations need not be complicated descriptions of how we wish our life to unfold or be corrected. The simpler they are, the more open ended will be the result, thereby allowing the greatest good to come to us. If we desire a specific thing, we need to affirm it as exactly as possible while using as few words as possible.

Simple affirmations play like melodies over and over as they repeat themselves in our minds. We want to be certain that these new seed thoughts take root in our minds and *reprogram our subconscious minds* to produce the outcomes we desire, uprooting and erasing any programs that conflict with the results we want. The easier our affirmations are to remember the more frequently we are apt to repeat them.

Conflicting Programs When we decide to pursue a certain line of thinking, perhaps to achieve a dream we have long cherished, it is common to find many obstacles in our way which are created by the old programs lying silently in our subconscious minds.

Until they are disturbed and revealed by our new ideas or dreams, they remain dormant. It is not until we consciously *reprogram the subconscious mind,* - our inner hard drive - that we see these old beliefs coming to the surface. Many people find these obstacles too forbidding and simply give up early in their efforts to make positive changes in their lives. However, it is not the *outside effort* that makes the difference but the *inside change of mind* we need to first put our focused energy into. Affirmations are an incredibly effective method for bringing about these changes.

Persist Conflicting programs often become entrenched in our internal hard drive as a result of a history of guilt. This could be due to past behavior we were not proud of or through early programming by parents that constantly berated us for our poor conduct while we were growing up. These influences produce programs of low self worth.

By affirming that we are a child of God or Universal Mind, one with All That Is, good and loving and abundant, we begin to uproot old patterns of unworthiness. The old programs will resist at first, perhaps fiercely, but persist and know that your new focus will win out and a new program, filled with positive possibilities will replace the lie that you were unworthy to receive your heart's desires, the lie that has held you back from receiving your birthright.

Affirming "Now" is Very Important When we affirm with a projected time factor that which we desire to manifest, we are *pushing it away from ourselves.* The reason is simple, projected goals separate our desire from us. The Universal Mind we live within is One, as such everything is One within It as It is One within everything. There is no time or separation in It.

Separation is the greatest cause of conflict there is, while unity forgives, binds and heals. Future time projection is by far the most common error in affirming a goal or dream. For this reason many people are disappointed with the results they have obtained using affirmations.

When we affirm our desires in the *now,* leaving time out of the scenario, we are saying to the subconscious mind, *"we already have this."* And in the unseen reality of thought, *it does exist.* The subconscious mind is our obedient servant and is our link to Universal Mind, All that Is or God. It takes our affirmative desire-thought and looks in it's vast database or memory bank for that which we have affirmed "we already have," and attracts to us the physical manifestation of it.

---

*"Many strokes. Though with a little axe, hew
down and fell the hardest timber's oak"*
Shakespeare

For example: If we say: *"I will be a millionaire two years from today,"* we have affirmed the good we desire is separate from us and at a considerable distance. You may be tempted to protest that this affirmation is both reasonable and realistic. However, if we say, *"I am a millionaire now,"* we are claiming what we desire has already occurred.

In the bible we are told to *"act as if it is already given to us."* The more we see and focus on that which we wish to bring forth, as if it has been given to us already, the faster it will begin to show up. Soon, so called *lucky* experiences or coincidences will begin to appear in our world. However, there are no coincidences and there is no such thing as luck.

Everything works according to Universal Law, *what we think about is what we see in our world.* Our conscious mind must recognize that on the unseen level, our desired outcome exists the moment we affirm it. Further, it must allow that Universal Mind or God to work in its "mysterious ways.

If we *tell* It what to do, It will fill the mold of our instructions, however these are usually limited in some way. But if we *allow* It to perform Its mysteries, so called luck appears everywhere, all the time. This is frequently referred to as a *miracle*, and seems to happen rarely for most people.

Yet the most natural things in the universe are *supernatural experiences* or what the world calls *miracles.* The truth is, it is *un-natural* when miracles do not occur. When we place our desire in the *now,* we are recognizing that it is ours, it exists in the unseen and *must* appear in manifest form. Universal Mind will provide the *how to* in Its mysterious ways, which are far better than anything we can conceive of, including *the when* of it.

Affirmations Must be 100% Positive In crafting our affirmations we must be careful to say them in a 100% positive manner.

For example, if we desire to get out of debt we should not mention debt or lack of finances at all. Remember, what we focus our attention upon expands. It is ironic that a well meaning desire to better our lives should have just the opposite effect if we allow the *idea of that condition* to enter our corrective statement.

An example of a self-defeating affirmation is: *"I am now completely debt free."* It is correctly spoken of in the present tense and has a confident commanding sound to it, however, it magnifies the condition we do not want - debt.

The correct affirmation would sound like this: *"I am financially independent now!"* It says much the same thing as the first example but focuses on the condition you *want* rather than the condition you *do not want.* We call this the *49% - 51% attitude.* It's a difference of only 2% but *if we shoot for the moon and miss by 2%, we are still lost in space.*

We believe affirmations are paramount in reprogramming our subconscious mind to help us create that which we desire. So important is the use of affirmations to help us to *think correctly* that we have included a summary of these points at the end of this chapter as a step by step process for creating *life-changing* affirmations for you.

Tell - Show - Try - Do

Simplicity is Genius -
"The lamp of genius burns quicker than the lamp of life"
Shiller

The Basics Mark Hughes was a master of simplicity. He used his humble beginnings as a banner for all to see that they too could replicate what he had done. He created *some of the most imitated phrases* found in business today.

For example his first and most famous slogan was: *"Lose Weight Now, Ask Me How"* The phrase *ask me how* has been added to the advertising tag lines of hundreds of different company's products following Mark's creation of the original slogan in 1980.

For his first promotion ever, he created a special program with qualifying sales volumes and a trip to Palm Springs for the winners to attend a special high level training and hear about the revolutionary advertising concept that would change the world. He made the event and the launch of his earth shaking concept sound and feel like the Academy Awards.

Though the sales force at the time was tiny, It didn't stop Mark from putting on this huge event. Everyone that was serious about the business *just had to qualify* for this Gala event. It turned out the event took place in a *rented house with a pool* where the qualifying distributors, enjoyed a weekend party and training hosted by Mark.

They shared sleeping facilities and made their own meals. He laid out his *world conquering plans* then rolled out the breakthrough advertising concept - the world shaking concept that Mark just couldn't wait to introduce. The reason for this huge gathering, was a metal button or badge that had the *"Lose Weight Now, Ask Me How"* slogan on it.

A less passionate dreamer would never have been able to pull it off, but Mark Hughes was a most passionate dreamer. His belief in Herbalife was translated into the affirmative power of this little slogan and button and has helped take Herbalife to the top of the weight loss industry worldwide.

Today the humble little button remains a staple in Herbalife's media toolbox. In fact many people equate *Herbalife and Lose Weight Now* as one and the same thing.

The person and the icon or symbol become inextricably intertwined with the quality of the spirit they achieved. Training was no different. *Complicated systems* for educating distributors meant *few people could duplicate them.*

Mark developed another catch phrase that once again, can still be found on the *tips of the tongues* of all successful distributors. If they were asked how to do the business their quick response would be: *"Use the Products - Where the Button - Talk to People"*

Mark could and often did expand this simple AFFIRMATION into an hour, a day or a weekend Extravaganza training and workshop, but always, the nucleus of the event was *Use-Wear-Talk.*

In this *simple mantra*, everyone could feel that if they just did a few simple things everyday, eventually they would achieve their dreams, they did, and still are.

"Simplicity of character is the natural result of profound thought"
Hazlitt

As the company grew and more and more people began realizing and surpassing their goals. Mark raised the pole and encouraged people to step into leadership roles so that he could duplicate himself and the company around the world.

He needed another AFFIRMATION and once again, simplicity was at its root. He wanted to show leaders how to create leaders and thereby duplicate the duplication process. So he created another affirmation called: *"Tell - Show - Try - Do"*

When translated this meant: *'Tell'* the new distributor *what to do*, then *'Show'* them *how to do it* yourself, then allow them to *'Try'* it *for themselves* and then they will *'Do'* it *on their own*. Once again, it became a catch phrase for teaching teachers to teach teachers.

None of these ideas are particularly NEW, but the manner in which Mark employed them so simply, and with such passion and excitement, was innovative and duplicable.

Duplication is the key to effortlessly and quickly manifesting successful outcomes. In some way, every process we see in our world for creating goods and services begins by teaching others to duplicate what we have done, then encouraging them to take it a step farther.

Mark's dream was to help teach everyone he came in contact with to do what he had done, whether it was simply improving their weight and health by taking the Herbalife products consistently, or through improving their financial status by duplicating his concept to teach teachers to take the Herbalife products around the world.

Creating Life Changing Affirmations

"Think you can, think you can't; either way, you'll be right"
Henry Ford

Specific Techniques That Work As we have explained above there is a definite process for creating life changing affirmations that are both simple and bring immediate results. Most people who utilize affirmations miss a few key ingredients and end up with very little success or create something other than what they originally desired.

Below is a summary of the steps for creating life-changing affirmations. Follow these simple steps and you will very quickly begin to experience powerful changes in your life.

Step One - Use Simplicity Create affirmations that are simple and easy to remember. One to two sentences are sufficient.

Step Two - Speak in the *first person generic statements.* Napoleon Hill's famous adage, *"What the mind of man can conceive and believe it can achieve,"* is a powerful statement of truth.

However, if you are applying it to yourself say, *"What I can conceive of, I believe and I effortlessly achieve."*

Step Three - Use Positive Language Create affirmations that speak *only* about what you desire and make no mention whatever about conditions you do not want.

For example: *"I will stop smoking within the next 30 days,"* speaks about the condition you do not want.

Universal Mind, remember is neutral and does not know or care that you have a positive objective. It will pour Its power into the mold you create and with this type of affirmation you are stimulating a condition that already exists - smoking - a condition that you do not want.

Instead you would say for example: *"I joyfully experience perfectly healthy breathing and I am now full of vitality."*

This focuses your attention on the condition you ultimately want and gives no power to the concept of smoking. If you pull the plug on the lamp called *"smoking"* and plug in the lamp called *"perfect breathing, perfect health and abundant vitality,"* one light goes out and the other light illuminates your world.

Step Four - Use the Present Tense Creating affirmations that say you will accomplish something in the future may feel logical, but Universal Mind knows nothing about time, everything is now.

Speaking in the future tense also validates the fact that your desire does not now exist in your world. This gives power to the condition you now have however this condition is *the one you wish to change.*

Instead of saying, "I will be driving a brand new red sports car by next spring," Say, *"I love the wonderful feeling and sense of freedom I have driving my red sports car now."*

Nevertheless, speaking in *the now* about future events can cause internal resistance that dilutes the emotional impact the affirmation has on your subconscious connection with Universal Mind and its power to manifest your desires .

To solve this challenge, if necessary, add a future date at the end of your affirmation written as if it is in the present tense. *"The date is now: January 1st, 20__ "(future date)."*

The tendency would be to say, "*I will have <u>such in such</u> by January 1st, 20__ (future date)."* However, once again, this validates that the desire is not now in your world. By saying the date is *"January 1st, 20__" (future date),"* you are saying that this future date is happening now.

Universal Mind *understands everything as now,* and to It, your desire is accomplished the moment you say it...in the unseen. It will *conspire* to provide *the ways and means* for your desire to manifest on the date you choose, but to It, that too needs to be brought into the now. Say the future day as if it were now. By doing this you are reinforcing your desired outcome.

Read this section as many times as necessary until it sinks in. This is an incredibly powerful aspect of effectively using affirmations to change your life.

Step Five - Use Emotional Words It important that you become *enthusiastic* about your desires. If your affirmations simply become *repetitive rote,* that do not capture your complete focused attention as you say them, the power they have to change your life will be minimal at best.

"I am thrilled to be living in my 5,000 square foot beachfront home enjoying beautiful weather. I feel comfortable, secure and satisfied in my dream home. The date is July 4th, 20__ (future date - spoken as if it is this very day)."

This is an exciting image and will soon bring many *synchronous events* into being that validate for you that *your dream home* is coming into your life on schedule.

Step Six - Self-Talk Visualization While every step is important, this last step is the most effective in bringing about immediate results.

This is how it works: While you repeat your affirmations, see and most important, *feel* the experience of your desire as if you were living it now. Get really excited!

As we mentioned in the chapter on Passion - a burning desire guided by love - has an irrepressible power to bring things into manifestation. *The fire of emotion* is the fuel that ignites your desire. By emotionally *feeling* your desired outcome while you speak it, *you turn on the engine of creation.*

How and When to Affirm When you say your affirmations speak them aloud wherever possible. The most effective times to repeat your affirmations are when you first wake up and when you are drifting off to sleep. This is because your brain is either in or is going into a frequency called * *alpha wave."*

This vibrational state of mind is conducive to the subconscious mind receiving input without the interference of the normal conscious *mind chatter"* that we experience during normal waking hours.

We suggest you commit your affirmations to memory so that you do not disturb this highly receptive state of mind. If your affirmation is connected to an emotionally charged desire, memorizing it will present no difficulty to you.

* *An excellent source of information on this subject can be found in "The Silva Mind Control Method," written by Jose Silva and available in most books stores.*

Summary

Miracles are a natural condition of life

1-   where we put our attention, both conscious and Subconscious, determines what we see in our world - anything is possible

Enthusiasm
(Motivation & Inspiration)

"Relaxed Intensity - The Art of Detached Passion"
John McIntosh

Mark's sensational productions became the mind-expanding force he used to lift attitudes into the stratosphere of possibilities

Inspiration versus Motivation

"Intuition is untaught ability"
Holmes

Motivation is an "Outside" Influence People, places and things that attract us, that get our attention, are in direct proportion to the level of *attractive energy* connected with them. Color, sound, movement, aroma, taste and texture all play on our emotions through our five basic senses and to the degree they excite our senses, we become *attentive.*

Continued exposure to high stimulation however, can actually stimulate our defenses to flare up against further contact with the sensation. *Energy sappers* turn us off. Everyone can recall an enthusiastic sales person whose intensity drained our energy, leaving us flat, defensive and irritable regardless of whether we bought what they were selling or not. Media commercials have the same effect on us.

Motivation is an outside influence that requires repeated trips to the well to quench our unending thirst. The source of motivation, being external in nature, necessitates a regular return to the well to continue benefiting from its enthusiastic and rejuvenating influence.

Tapes, CD's, videos, workshops, books and personal counseling are outside sources or aides we have all subscribed to at one time at or another. These forms of mental, emotional and physical stimulation have been highly popular for much of the last century and have had their place in urging us toward Self-Empowerment and Self-Discovery.

However, in the last 15 years, Self-Discovery has grown exponentially around the world as people ask:

"What's it all about...?"

This primal question cannot be answered from outside sources for at least two reasons.

Firstly, as mentioned, the outside source is not always readily available when the urge to understand our purpose for living nudges our mind. And second, because the quality of the information from an outside source is just that, outside, limited and biased. It is subjective and colored by the personal opinions and beliefs of the source providing it.

It is impossible for the motivation to be perfectly aligned with our personal needs. No matter how lofty the role models may be, they have their own bridges to cross which means the guidance that comes through them must pass through *the rose colored glass of their baggage*, bringing with it their own *unhealed issues*.

Inspiration is an Inside - Self-Empowering Influence As a result, there is now occurring a subtle shift from *motivation to inspiration* as this worldwide inner search gains momentum. Inspiration uses the benefits of outside motivation to lead a person inward for answers that are pure, personal and always available. It is a process of leading the horse to the water. Once we reach the water, we choose just how much we desire to drink, but *it is we* who do the drinking ourselves.

"Inspiration and genius - one and the same thing"
Victor Hugo

As the urge grows, motivational enthusiasm changes to inspirational intensity. And as we listen, comprehend and follow the pristine and timely guidance from within, we become peacefully aware that the fears we thought were real do not exist and the mountains we thought insurmountable are easily moved.

This state of mind adds a relaxed feeling to our ever-growing sense of inner knowing. The intensity we now experience is *more passionate yet relaxed*, unattached to possible outcomes because we have learned that everything works out for our highest purpose as we listen for and yield to our own personal inner guidance.

"No man was ever great without a touch of divine inspiration"
Cicero

We can all recall being in the company of someone who was obviously passionate about his interests in life but totally neutral about whether we joined him in his excitement. In other words he did not rely on our approval or acceptance to stay intensely passionate about his dreams. Comparing temporary enthusiasm to *relaxed intensity* is like comparing *the sun to a match.*

Larger Than Life

"Nothing great was ever achieved without enthusiasm"
Ralph Waldo Emerson

Enthusiasm - the Genius of Sincerity To say that Mark Hughes was enthusiastic was like saying water is wet. Without a single word or movement of body language you could feel the energy of enthusiasm radiating from him.

And, to ask if Mark motivated others to become enthusiastic is to ask if fire could boil water. Everyone became electrified around him and like all great motivators, he provided the external tools to keep them *charged.* An abundant supply of videos, tapes, satellite broadcasts faxes, emails, conference calls, literature, promotional vacations and extravaganzas flowed to his distributors.

His sense of timing and ability to read an audience's energy was impeccable. Because he had his entire body, mind and spirit tuned to the pulse of an audience, he knew exactly how to raise its frequency to a fever pitch.

A Flair for the Theatrical Mark also had a theatrical flair for high drama. In one large function at which distributors from around the world were in attendance, the house lights were dimmed and a huge screen showed a close up of Mark in a helicopter flying over the conference center we were all gathered in. It looked as if it was live coverage of what was actually happening.

We watched the helicopter descend toward the roof of the building and once again the lights went down. At that point it sounded like the helicopter was in the room with us.

A few moments later the lights came back up and there was Mark stepping out of a helicopter which was sitting on the stage. The crowd went wild and the elation that filled the room at that moment remained until Mark finished his lecture.

Grand Thinking Those of us that knew Mark personally were aware of a deeper motive for his sensational showmanship. We understood the motivational value of showmanship and how it riveted everyone's attention on Mark's every word. But few knew his primary objective was to instill an attitude of *grand thinking* into his distributors.

"Enthusiasm is faith in action"
Henry Chester

The *over-the-top performance* was the hallmark of Mark Hughes and became so common that everyone of us expected that with Herbalife, everything was larger than life, everything was possible,

Thinking "Outside" the Box Mark wanted his distributors to focus their attention outside the box of conventional thinking. Conventionally accepted thinking tells the world that for some people, there are limitations to what they can achieve - and that's just the way it is.

"Enthusiasm is at the bottom of all progress"
Henry Ford

If Mark was to take Herbalife around the world, he knew he needed distributors to *think worldwide* and to *think without limitations* restricting their desires. His mind may have been on many subjects at a time within the framework of his dream, but he was confined to one body and he knew he needed many distributors to emerge as leaders, and step up to the plate to join arms with him, if he was to accomplish his vision.

---

*"Enthusiasm spells the difference between
mediocrity and accomplishment"*
Norman Vincent Peale

Never was this more important than in the area of remuneration. To expand the average person's belief so that their *previous yearly income* became a *believable monthly income* required far more than just a mathematical formula that explained what was possible on paper.

Big incomes required major sales volumes and resulted in major corporate growth. This meant that minds atrophied by the philosophy of 9-5, 40 years and a pension, had to be *jump started* by a new and *larger-than-life vision*.

Mark's sensational productions therefore became the mind-expanding force he used to lift attitudes into the stratosphere of possibilities. He held parties with stars like Wayne Newton, Milton Berle, the Osmonds, Paul Anka, Bob Newhart and Rod Stewart to name a few.

He created promotions such as, *"The Cruise with Hughes"* where he bought an entire luxury cruise ship for a week and toured the Caribbean with Herbalife adorning the sides of the ship. He orchestrated bonus vacations to the very best resorts worldwide for hundreds of qualifying distributors - every year. He gave away a Rolls Royces for the #1 distributor for a number of years.

And, he threw parties at his Beverly Hills Mansion that rivaled Gala's at the White House. *It was impossible to have limited thinking* after being constantly exposed to one incredible promotion after another.

Paradigm Shift Mark also joined the handful of motivational leaders who were making the shift into the field of Self Empowerment through inspiration by hiring Jim Rohn. Jim had been a world-renowned speaker for fortune 500 companies for decades and Mark knew that introducing Jim to his dream would be a marriage made in heaven.

This union would help bring about a harvest of leaders that thought for themselves and marched to their own drumbeat. Jim had been very visible with the company and appeared at many functions for Herbalife since 1987, but Mark wanted him on staff.

In the mid 90's he finally persuaded Jim to help take his dream around the world and motivation was coupled with inspiration to round out the steady positive molding of the minds and character of thousands of up-and-coming leaders.

"We can have more than we've got because we can become more than we are"
Jim Rohn

Summary

Inner guided inspiration generates enthusiastic intensity

1-	enthusiasm generated by outside motivation is temporary and unreliable

2-	enthusiasm inspired from within is solid and completely dependable promoting a sense of peace and relaxed intensity

Discipline
(Consistency + Persistence)

"Great thoughts reduced to practice become great acts"
William Hazlitt

"If you were the boss of your own company, would you fire yourself?"

Removing Obstacles

*"The human spirit is stronger than anything
that can happen to it"*
George C. Scott

We Create our own Obstacles When we become clear that we create our own reality through the power of our thoughts impressed upon the infinite field of possibilities, or Universal Mind, we are well on our way to living our lives in joy, peace, abundance and love. However, creation is not linear in nature.

Creation follows the path of least resistance and will wind itself around any obstacle to achieve its intention.

Let us explore the subject of obstacles. In reality, we have placed these blocks or delays on our path in the way of our desires. We may not remember placing them there, but place them there, *we did.*

Sometimes what we placed in our way on the path in some distant past is highly beneficial to our progress.

If we are driving from New York to Los Angeles without the benefit of a road map, the result could be detrimental, as we end up taking side roads, by- ways and detours on the way to our destination.

The journey may be fraught with challenges, yet we will still achieve our objective by simply persisting and heading southwest. Nevertheless, with the aid of a road map obtained before we leave, our journey will be far easier and allow us to enjoy the trip as we go.

Notwithstanding, more often than not what we created in the past was a *series of roadblocks.*

By far one of the most common roadblocks is *a lack of discipline.* We describe discipline as a combination of consistency and persistence.

Instant Results Once we have chosen the objective of our desire based on our life purpose; we must make it our constant focus, keeping it steadily before our mind's eye. If there were no obstacles in our way, we would literally see our dreams manifest before our eyes instantly. Most would accurately call this a miracle.

While most people do not experience the instant manifestation of their desires, consistent persistence in removing the blocks to the flow of one's desires dramatically increases the speed with which results occur.

This is at the heart of *spontaneous healing.* The removal of blocks to the power of love's presence heals *all obstacles,* including physical, financial, and emotional and any aspect of our lives, which is not whole.

Let us say for now that we, like most people, still have several blocks in the way of instant manifestation of our dreams. And further, let us agree we probably do not know what many of these blocks are. How do we overcome them and create our dreams?

Rainwater does not struggle to fall from the clouds; it simply allows the law of gravity to perform its task. Our task is not *how to* bring our dreams into reality; our task is to determine *what* our dreams are then consistently persist in focusing our thoughts upon them.

"What" is Your Job - "How" belongs to Universal Mind

The magnetic quality of thoughts will find its way around any and all obstacles that may exist or that we may have created for ourselves in the past, and attract to us the people, places, circumstances and things we require to bring our dreams into reality.

This is the *how to* of creation. It is not our concern and yet most people focus on this aspect of creation almost to the exclusion of *what* they desire. Our task is to discover *what* our true desires are then apply our *undivided attention* or *disciplined focus* upon them.

"A straight path never leads anywhere except to the objective"
Andre Gide

As we discussed earlier, our true desires will be found in our life purpose.
If we have found our life's purpose and as a by-product, passion to achieve it has bubbled to the surface, our belief in our dreams is self-evident; it is already a part of our being.

The belief we must foster is in the efficacy of the law. We must believe that Universal Mind will take care of the *how to*. This is the key ingredient. Obeying this law as we would any physical law means we discipline ourselves to be consistently persistent, keeping that belief-thought constantly in the forefront of our mind as a partner to our desire focus.

Our focused thought then will end up where unto it is directed naturally and effortlessly. It will find the ways and means - *the how to* - by mysterious and wonderful means because this law is an aspect of the omniscience of the field of infinite possibilities or Universal Mind. We do our part by being *consistently persistent or vigilant for our life purpose or dream*.

This is true because our life's purpose always seeks to serve all in love and as such is in divine harmony with Universal Mind which is all inclusive or Whole.

This is truly serving God or divine purpose. As we do this we fulfill the edict to *"seek first the kingdom"* or be *"in unity"* with the One mind back of all creation.

When we follow this wise direction the ways and means to fulfill our dreams, and fully actualize our life purpose is given to us precisely *when* it is needed, often in wonderful and amazing ways.

"God works in mysterious ways, His wonders to perform."
William Cowper &
Psalm 77:11-14

Realizing our need for consistent and persistent focused thought in order to bring our dreams into manifestation, we may wish to consider making the habit of discipline one of our first objectives if we have not already done so.

Daily Method of Operation "DMO"

"If you are facing in the right direction, all you need to do is keeping on walking"
Buddhist Proverb

Hire Yourself As we have said, Mark used simple concepts that anyone could duplicate, in that way finding people to help him build his dream was relatively easy. The master key was to take these POWER KEYS, wrap them around the focused attention of his dream and teach people to place their daily focus on the same things.

He called this concept the *"Daily Method of Operation or DMO"* for short. He encouraged everyone to discover their own purpose or dream then place it in the vehicle that he created - Herbalife - and practice a few simple principles everyday.

He used to ask people:

"If you were the boss of your company, would you fire yourself?"

Naturally, this question would elicit great laughter, but he would then become serious and go on to say: *"Hey guys, ya need to hire yerself. Most of you are used to regular jobs and daily routines. Ya won''t know what to do with the freedom ya have when ya work for yerself...if ya don't get into a daily method of operation."*

After that he would review all he had taught hundreds of times before, the barest of daily basics like: *"Use the Products, Wear the Button, Talk to People."*

Simple Repetition In this way he successfully illustrated how the consistent and persistent employment of a simple DMO over time resulted in financial freedom, and that the people demonstrating this were no different than the newer distributors that had just begun achieving a little success doing these identical things every day.

"The waters wear the stones"
Job 14:19

Mark's concepts were always simple and consistent. He taught that a few basic disciplines practiced *"EVERY...SINGLE...DAY..."* would eventually achieve incredible results. *"EVERY...SINGLE...DAY..."* was one of his most frequently used phrases.

Like many of his simple sayings, it was a chant that helped train the minds of people who had been used to working for someone else and being given instructions on what, when and how to do their jobs. Gradually this simple method helped these people become *self managed* and over time, led many people to high levels of self empowerment.

Summary

Universal Mind provides the "ways and means"
to accomplish your Life Purpose

1-   "what" we desire is our function, "how to" attain it is the function of the Universal Mind as shown to us by our Inner Guidance

2-   we need only persist consistently in the direction given from within to attain "what" we desire

Humor

"Laughter is the best medicine"
Norman Cousins

Mark took every opportunity to bring levity into his business without minimizing the importance of his mission

The Heart of a Healer

All people laugh in the same language"
Anon

Laughter Heals Most of us feel lighter when exposed to laughter. True humor ignites laughter that wounds no one yet minimizes the anxious importance we place on transitory things.

We are such a serious people, we humans. Our wrinkled foreheads and stern countenances mirror the value we place on things that are here today and gone tomorrow. Famous comedians often use the human intensity found in our daily newspapers as raw material for their humor. They help us to laugh at our foolish behavior and thereby gain a clearer perspective of what really counts.

In recent years medical science journals have been full of studies done on the positive effects humor and laughter have on the immune system.

"The joyfulness of a man prolongs his days"
Ecclesiastics 30:22.

For this reason alone one might consider taking a moment to read the comics, follow the joke of the day in the newspaper, or watch the silly antics of a sitcom for thirty minutes. You might want to pick up the movie *"Patch Adams"* for excellent visible proof of this truth.

More than this, we should take a careful inventory of *what is so important* that *it takes away our peace.* It is very easy to connect responsibility with excessive seriousness. With this attitude an easy going, carefree, lighthearted attitude can be mistaken for recklessness.

Joyful Abundance Recently we watched a well known television personality, Charlie Rose interview Richard Branson, President of Virgin Atlantic Airlines and several other worldwide enterprises.

We had seen Mr. Branson a number of times in the press and were intrigued by his contagious smile and by his phenomenal achievements in a variety of diverse areas. What struck us most about the interview was his joy for living.

"A merry heart makes a cheerful countenance"
English Proverb

Branson's life is an incredible adventure - from terrifying balloon flights, record breaking Atlantic crossings, court-room battles with British Airways to the daring Gulf War airlift from Baghdad and the sale of the world-famous Virgin Records.

Next he's planning commercial flights into outer space - hundreds have already reserved their seat at 10's of thousands of dollars each.

This man lives on the edge every moment of his life, in fact he lives *in the moment.* Consciously living *in the moment.* Is living *in the now* where the past and future have no fearful meaning and provides us with no point of reference. In this state we simply allow our inner guidance to direct us to our highest possibilities in every moment.

How could the fear of the past intrude on an attitude like that? Branson is a man that breaks into an infectious smile when faced with confrontation.

Imagine how he handles cooperation. Yet, Branson is a man juggling a multitude of business enterprises. No doubt, he is absolutely serious and focused upon his business interests but he obviously does not allow them to steal his joy.

To live this way, with a light heart, a face that is quick to break into a bright smile and an attitude that breeds joy in every situation is contagious, attractive and magnetic to creative circumstances coming into our lives.

"Among people who hate, let us live in love"
The Dhammapada

People like this help empower our lives and our work and lift our souls to new heights. Laughter, joy and light heartedness bring love to hate and healing to hurt. It bridges divisions and like music, knows no boundaries. It is the fruit of heavenly seed and blesses everyone it touches.

Let us think now of the feelings we have when we experience the completely innocent laughter of a baby. Few things fill the heart more; few things curl the lips and brighten the eyes more easily. Few things bring us this close to God.

"Laugh and the world laughs with you,
weep and you weep alone"
Ella Wheeler Wilcox

The Power of Laughter

"A look filled with understanding, an accepting smile, a loving word, a meal shared in warmth and awareness are the things which create happiness in the present moment'
Thich Nhat Hanh

A Child Leads I cannot think of anyone I know that fell so easily into laughter at every opportunity. Mark was the most serious while at the same time, joyfully lighthearted person I ever knew. He could be totally focused and in the same moment detached, not indifferent, just uncontrolled by outcomes.

And there was no lapse of time between a happy or sad incident and Mark's reaction to it. He would weep just as quickly as he would burst out in uproarious laughter.

In this respect his heart was open, he allowed himself to be joyously vulnerable. The greater his accomplishments and closer his dream, the more open, smiling and available his spirit became.

He would use any opportunity to bring large ideas down to bite sized concepts that anyone could digest easily. On one occasion during the initial launch phase of Herbalife's natural skin care division, Dermajetics, Mark took the opportunity to parody himself and the products by dancing to the song: *"I'm too sexy for my..."* The routine looked like something out of a Saturday Night Live sketch and took all of us completely off guard.

We melted into joyous laughter until our sides ached. Mark himself was in tears from laughing so hard.

Lightness Lifts Large Weights He would also use humor to disarm touchy subjects. For instance, highly successful distributors in the company were also highly visible and certain to be considered role models for thousands of distributors around the world.

"We must laugh and we must sing, we are blest by everything"
W. B. Yeats

On one occasion, I was with my friend Alan Lorenz who at the time was the number one distributor in the world. We were at a garden party at Mark's Maui estate and Mark was standing near us.

The party was in a beautiful tropical setting so I asked Mark and Alan if I could take a picture of the two of them together. Mark and Alan were a blessing to the most aggressive Paparazzi; they loved to have their pictures taken. They immediately posed for me, in front of some palm trees with the ocean as a backdrop.

Alan was dressed in swim trunks and a tight T-shirt that nicely displayed his round little belly for the camera. Mark had his arm around Alan's shoulder and looked down at the offending protrusion. He began giggling and chided his friend, *"Suck in Alan!"* Alan immediately complied as he and Mark began giggling along with a crowd of onlookers.

It was an opportune time to gently nudge his top distributor into displaying a better image of the value of using the products, without centering him out or wounding him. The next time I saw Alan, about a month later, the paunch was gone.

"One joy scatters a hundred griefs"
Chinese Proverb

Joyful Work - Joyful Play Mark took every opportunity to bring levity into his business without minimizing the importance of his mission. He would take over an entire theme park like Disney for his distributors for an evening. He would create theme parties at large Herbalife events that required everyone to show up in costume.

Fifties nights and twenties - gangster themes were favorites of Mark's. On another occasion Mark orchestrated a sailing regatta around an island in Hawaii using genuine *"American Cup"* replica boats. The event ended with a massive water-rifle battle. It was like watching group of grade school children lose themselves in joyful abandon.

"Joy is the realization of oneness, the oneness of our soul with the world and of the world-soul with the supreme love"
Tagore

At corporate vacations Mark could be found wildly drawing on a whiteboard in a highly competitive game of Pictionary or fiercely defending the net in a game of water polo. If a casual passerby were to watch him at play they would never suspect he was the CEO of a multi billion-dollar international empire.

"Every day is my best day, this is my life. I'm not going to have this moment again."
Dr. Bernie Siegel

Not long after Mark passed away, my friend Jim Rohn sadly shared with me: *"Mark should have gotten double his 44 years."* I agreed, but we both knew that in his brief life, Mark Hughes lived each day fully and abundantly as if it was his last and always lived with humor, laughter and joy.

Summary

Life is in the moment

1-   by living "in the moment" or "in the now" we prevent our past from dictating our future

2-   this eliminates fear and promotes a lighthearted attitude that fosters the healing power of love

Adaptability

and

Innovation

---

*"If you do not change direction you will end up
where you are headed"*
Lao Tzu

"We jumped into the limo and there was Mark comfortably slumped in the back seat. He threw up his hands as if to indicate 'oh well,' and said, "Well, that didn't work...next!""

Failure Is Not An Option

"A person will make more opportunities than he finds"
Francis Bacon

Nature Knows No Defeat Life is organic and tenaciously follows its innate understanding of the path of least resistance. If there is a rock in the path of a root's search for nourishment it simply continues around it patiently. If on the other hand the same plant is growing under an asphalt road, it will hunt for a weak spot and irrepressibly punch a hole through the obstruction to the life giving sunlight it seeks.

Life will fly before it builds bridges, it will build bridges before it hikes around broken pathways, but it *will* do whatever is required in order for it to grow and extend itself through reproduction, because it adapts through innovation.

"There are only two ways to live your life, one is as though nothing is a miracle and the other is as if everything is a miracle"
Albert Einstein

Anyone who has made even a cursory study of Nature has witnessed an amazing while unidentified creative genius intelligence at work. This intelligence has one huge advantage over the average human being; it does not recognize the presence of limitations. Erosion can take hundreds of years to smooth obstructive rock. Thousands of seedlings may die in order for *one* to grow into the fullness of life.

The nature of Nature is to think as one. And, it thinks as one unit despite it's many parts, shedding facets of itself like dead skin in order for the whole to survive and flourish.

Nature does not recognize failure on its onward push to grow and thrive and express the divine image hidden within it. It has no say in the matter; it must obey the laws of the Universal Mind within itself never knowing anything about choice. The chameleon does not sit and *figure out* what color to change its skin into, it just obeys the divine instinct within and immediately adapts.

Free Will Human beings are the only species that are endowed with the gift of free will. As such we consider our options, then we decide through choice what road to take.

For many people these choices are prompted by outside considerations and require a long arduous and usually painful analysis to achieve even modest results. Herein lies the source of our suffering.

We have an inner drive that urges us to press on and express the highest within, but we often fail to accept the inner guidance advice within that prompts us toward the path of least resistance, the path of our highest purpose.

The world we live in is swiftly changing and simplicity is at last being given its due recognition. Adjusting to change through inner directed guidance and growing through innovation provided by this Divine source is lightening quick and always uses the path of least resistance.

"The struggle to learn to listen to and respect our own intuitive, inner promptings is the greatest challenge of all"
Herb Goldberg

Look Within The outside world is not a prerequisite for successfully adapting our dreams and making them a reality. Looking within means keeping our inner eye focused on what we desire with all the passion the attainment of our dreams requires. In this dedicated focus we will be inspired by Universal Mind, our own inner guide.

This intelligence, this field of infinite possibilities within us will provide the perfect direction, the exact methods and the precise innovation we require at the right moment, every moment.

If you observe the seemingly magical performance of a top athlete you may catch them silently watching for the signal to proceed. This is the *cue* that comes from their inner guide. This is the inner intelligence that helps create the *superstar that one who stands out in the crowd* who wins the trophy at the end of the season.

"[inner] Self trust is the first secret of success"
Ralph Waldo Emerson

This is typical of what is possible when we listen to the voice within. Many call this space, *the zone.* We call it intuition, gut feelings, hunches or insights. You may have a different name for it, whatever feels right for you, but its essence is inner guided. This essence emanates from the highest aspect of our Self, Universal Mind or God.

"What we need are more people who specialize in the impossible"
Theodore Roethke

It is the same adaptability and spirit of innovation that has guided nature to evolve and grow effortlessly for eons. We have this gift, this great power within all of us. We need only chose to tap into it and listen. It will lead us to the path of least resistance.

Turning Disaster Into Advantage

"Trouble creates a capacity to handle it"
Oliver Wendell Holmes, Jr.

Lemons into Lemonade In a later chapter we speak in more detail about a Gala event in Orlando that *nearly sunk the company*. This story is a fascinating example of Mark Hughes' ability to adapt to change and challenge and use it to innovate new and valuable ideas.

Two friends of mine, Phil and Debbie Blurton, were among a small group of distributors known as, *The Sixth Graders*. These were Herbalife distributors who had attended grade school with Mark Hughes.

Phil and Debbie and I were in attendance at this particular event in Orlando. Just before the black tie dinner was to begin in a huge tent, the floor began to collapse into a sinkhole. After Phil and Debbie departed the sinking tent along with a hundred other traumatized guests, all dressed in formal attire; they trudged up a long steep red carpet to the transportation waiting to return them to the hotel.

Mark spotted them and invited them to return to the hotel in his limousine. I recall with such delight, Phil, laughing while shaking his head in wonder, as he explained this story to me. Mark paid the occurrence, which had cost just under a million dollars to stage, little mind. He didn't focus on what others might have seen.

"We jumped into the limo and there was Mark comfortably slumped in the back seat. He threw up his hands as if to indicate "oh well," and said: "Well, that didn't work...next!""

He saw it as an opportunity to fire up his creative genius. It was a tool, an instrument for furthering his dream. He was not attached to it, he knew it could be replaced, as it turned out with something better.

As the deeply shaken guests arrived back at the hotel, they found a new event had already been staged for them. Cases of Dom Perignon champagne had been salvaged from the *sink-hole-tent-party* and a couple of hundred Dominoes pizzas had been ordered and brought back to a hastily orchestrated *"Dom and Dom party."*

"Do the things you think you cannot do"
Eleanor Roosevelt

The mood changed from Gala fiasco to joyful abandon. Everyone relaxed immediately and enjoyed the best party Herbalife had ever staged for them. Mark milked the success of this on-the-spot innovative idea and made the *"Dom & Dom party"* a regular event for the next few years.

On another occasion a small group of us were attending an intimate training with Mark in Kauai, Hawaii. These events were working vacations and allowed us to relax, play and brainstorm under simply gorgeous conditions. I know Mark looked forward to these fun filled "think tank" sessions as much as we did in the early years of Herbalife's growth.

Shift Gears During the middle of speaking one day Mark got an urgent call that Mexico, which had only recently opened, had been shut down for some unknown reason. We never saw Mark at the event after that. He had hopped the first flight to Mexico to attend to the matter personally and immediately. He was able to shift gears in mid stream and re-focus his attention elsewhere because he understood the need to adapt.

In this situation with the Mexican government it took Mark nearly an entire year to innovate a new deal. But he had taken the stance that it was possible to adapt immediately to what was required to stay in the country, and he acted on that assumption.

He always struck while the iron was hot. *Think back to the most memorable and heavenly times you have had in your life. Were they organized or did they "just happen?" This is the way inner guidance works. It adapts and innovates on the spot, exactly what is perfect for our highest purpose.*

Things didn't always work out right away, sometimes challenges took considerable time to work out, as in the Mexico issue, but they would never have worked out if he had taken the attitude that they wouldn't.

He believed all challenges could be solved and for the most part, he believed this was possible right away. He used to say, *"If somthin can be done, why not right now?"* In addition, Mark always took the attitude, *"in the midst of difficulty - opportunity lurked."*

Mark not only employed the attitude of immediate adaptability with virtually any challenge but also in innovating new concepts to fit his far reaching vision. He knew that if he was going to successfully take his dream around the world, Herbalife would need to have a world class image in nutritional weight management. For that reason his focus always included cutting edge research in the scientific development of products.

An offspring of this long term innovative attitude and focus was the product launch in the early 90's of Thermojetics. While the concept of burning fat and thermogenesis was not new to nutritional science, the masses had never heard of it. The Thermojetics line of products became the icon for weight loss in the 90's and one of the most imitated catchall phrases by lesser-known weight loss companies, which had ever been.

"Imitation is the highest form of flattery"

If this is true, Herbalife was the most admired company of that era. For Herbalife, Thermojetics helped create a tidal wave of growth that took Herbalife around the world as Mark had dreamed.

"100% of the *shots you don't take, do not go in!"*
Wayne Gretzky

Summary

*Living your Life Purpose successfully requires
Adaptability*

1-   life does not travel in a straight line; we must always be ready to change direction, as the need requires

2-   only by following the direction from within will we know "when" changes are needed and "how to" adapt to them

Single Minded Focus

"Your life becomes what you think"
Marcus Aurelius

Mark Hughes exemplified the classic success minded trait of single-minded focus. When he got something into his mind it was already a "done deal"

Thinking Makes It So

"There is nothing either good or bad, but thinking makes it so."
William Shakespeare

Change Your Mind - Change Your World Above and beyond all experience, education, social status, special connections, physical health, or any circumstance we may be in right now, thought shines as the supreme instrument of change.

What do we see every day in our life? Whatever it is, we see it because we expect to see it. As we give constant thought to our expectations, they remain in our life and expand into other areas of our life.

"Thoughts are things"
Charles Fillmore

Let's say we have chosen to radically change our life. We break up a relationship, leave our job, move to another town and begin our life anew. However, unless we change the *cause or the thought process* behind the life we were leading, within months we will have duplicated every aspect of it.

The names, places and faces may look different (although not necessarily) but the essence behind them will be identical to the life we thought we left behind. We continually see the effects of what *we are thinking pressed out into our world*. Over and over again, we recreate what we have experienced before - unless we change our thoughts.

Like many people, we may be completely unaware of the power we have within ourselves to make our world exactly the way you wish it to be. We may have a tendency to blame other people, other conditions and other circumstances for the way our life is playing out each day. However, right this moment we have the ability to shape and mold our life exactly as we desire it to be through the use of our focused thoughts.

Once we become aware that *we really do have this power* to draw to us everything we desire, it will become clear that we must be careful about the thoughts we allow to flow continuously through our minds.

As this occurs it will soon become habitual for us to watch our feelings and the thoughts they bring up throughout the day. We will become a witness as well as an active participant in our own life. In this way we will begin to see the link between the thoughts we have and the way those thoughts are reflected in our life. *"Wherever you go, there you are"*

Focus = Power The more focused our thoughts are the more power they have to attract their mirror image into our life. A casual wish is like a wisp of wind that quickly loses its vitality and disappears into the ocean of thoughts that float throughout Universal Mind. Some thoughts are neutralized by other thoughts we have had which contradict the core idea of those thoughts.

For example, if we have a desire-thought to improve our position in the company in which we work but we also have an underlying thought-program that says we never get a break, our new thought will not likely come to successful fruition.

"No man can serve two masters"
Matthew 6:24

To remedy this all too common challenge, this and any contradictory underlying thought-program can be overwritten with new and positive thought-programs through the power of affirmations.

(Please refer to the chapter on "Simplicity and Affirmations" for the process to create life changing affirmations)

Like most people, we have all likely experienced periodic flashes of inspiration to change and improve our lives only to have those inspirations dashed on the rocks of procrastination shortly after we begin to think about them.

We have all heard about people who want to improve the appearance and vitality of their bodies and soon afterward can be found with brand new exercise machines they bought through an infomercial *they just happened to see on television."* A week or two later, the machine is collecting dust under the bed.

"Stamp indelibly on your mind a mental picture of yourself succeeding. Hold onto this picture tenaciously. Never permit it to fade. Your mind will seek to develop it"
Norman Vincent Peale

Like Attracts Like Spotting the infomercial was not a coincidence, it was the magnetic attractive power of thought in action. The desire-thought to improve their body attracted a possible method of fulfilling it.

To further illustrate this magnetic influence, watch what happens when you drive away from the dealership after purchasing a new automobile. Within hours, it seems every other car on the road is identical to the one you just bought.

The principle is the same with the TV commercial. The desire-thought tuned into a certain frequency, just like a radio channel and the exercise machine commercial appeared. If we persist in sending out any desire-thought, our link with Universal Mind will continually attract people, things and circumstances to us that are in harmony with the desire-thought.

But why did the person buying the exercise machine fail to follow through? Because, other thought-programs neutralized the new exercise desire-thought. For example, they may have thought-programs in their mind that says, *"I've tried things like this before and they never worked out."*

"All that we are is a result of what we have thought"
Buddha

All other desire-thoughts that failed to manifest in the past did so for the same reason. Each unsuccessful desire-thought that is tuned in to that particular channel of failure reinforces and expands that *self defeating thought-program."* And the process continues on and on by influencing every new desire-thoughts we have that vibrates at that same frequency.

Overcoming Self-Defeating Programs These *self-defeating* thought-programs have to do with a sense of unworthiness. To overcome *self-defeating* programs we must over-write these thought-programs with new *supportive* thought-programs.

By building a thought-program that relays constant messages of self worth to our subconscious mind, every desire-thought we sow into our subconscious-hard-drive will be automatically nurtured, allowing it to come to successful fruition in our everyday life. Once again, affirmations hold the power to over-write offending thought-programs with new and supportive thought-programs.

> *"It is not enough to have a good mind.*
> *The main thing is to use it well."*
> **Rene Descartes**

Affirm Success Here is a simple and powerful affirmation you may consider saying to yourself several times a day. If you try this affirmation, within a few days you will begin to notice a definite change in your sense of well being because the natural state for all of us is one of peace.

"I am at one with the all loving creative universe. I live and have my being in this ocean of abundance. This abundance is everywhere and all around me; in fact it IS me. Since abundance IS me I am already worthy to receive it. I open myself up to receive what is already mine. I now receive with gratitude the abundance that I am."

A profound feeling of peace to enter your daily life when you know that your every need is within your grasp, simply by allowing it to come forth from within yourself.

> *"In the beginning was the Word, and the Word was with God, (Universal Mind) and the Word was God."*
> **John 1:1**

Mankind is a part of this Word and we have the same power to create through it as in the beginning. It is neutral and will mirror back to us whatever we *speak-think into* it.

All focused thought, when persisted in, will produce after its kind. This is a Universal Law. The Word-thought manifests in the material world. To understand this is to accept responsibility for everything that happens in our life. When we accept this responsibility we chose our thoughts carefully before we focus on them.

Choose Your Thoughts Carefully As we have said, choosing our thoughts carefully involves over-writing the thought-programs that dilute or contaminate the pure thoughts we seek to see manifest in our world.

"We choose our joys and sorrows
long before we experience them"
Kahlil Gibran

However, to discover and root out the multitude of these offending thought programs is well beyond our conscious capacity. To accomplish this formidable task, we must call on the inner guide that knows the *perfect pattern* for our highest purpose. The procedure is simple, effective and thorough. Here is an affirmation you may wish to use to accomplish this task.

"Within me now is the perfect pattern for my highest good. I call on this perfect pattern to filter out any thought-programs that are not in perfect harmony with my highest good. I give thanks that is done now."

Using this affirmation regularly will *purify* the slate of your subconscious mind and allow you to focus your desire-thoughts without the interference of offending negative thought-programs. What you will bring forth into your life will then reflect accurately what you think about consciously.

We have the power to *think our life into what we would have it be*. What will you do now that you know that you can do anything?

" Nothing is separate from the mind that creates it"
Ananda

Energy Follows Thought

"For one who has conquered the mind,
the mind is the best of friends"
Bhagavad Gita

Unswerving Focus Mark Hughes exemplified the classic success minded trait of single-minded focus. When he got something into his mind it was already a *done deal* in his mind. His circumstances merely had to *catch up* with his focused thought. The essence or spirit of Mark's dream was already accomplished.

"You must think as would the person you want to become."
Earl Nightingale

One New Year's Eve, Mark was in Las Vegas with a few of his closest friends in Herbalife. Since Herbalife was his family, that is where most of his friends could be found. He was playing at a baccarat table with Marcus Lehmann, one of Herbalife's top distributors. Marcus states: *"I know these games very well, but Mark was an amateur. He seemed to play almost recklessly, but had incredible luck!"*

As we have already stated, Universal Mind is exact, *energy follows thought.* And everything that occurs does so because thought preceded it. The more powerful and focused the thought and the deeper the belief that underpins it, the quicker and more certain the manifestation will be of the thought. Luck does not have a hand in how this world plays out.

"Once you make a decision (to do something), the world
conspires to make it happen"
Ralph Waldo Emerson

Mark and Marcus had been playing for some time when they decided to cash out their winnings. Mark gave his chips to the cashier and discovered he had won just under a million dollars. Mark was extremely visual in creating his dreams, so you can imagine how the million dollar mark might immediately have a striking impression on his sense of focus.

He took one look at Marcus, grinned, and Marcus knew they were heading back to the tables. It was not long before Mark was down considerably, but the money was not the issue, the target of a million dollars was the focus. And, you guessed it, Mark made the mark!

Relaxed- Focused- Intensity When he got an *inspiration* to accomplish something his mind became riveted on it and did not leave it until the thought manifested.

Whether it was creating a safe and natural product for the health of the cardiovascular system (because heart disease was the biggest killer in America), finding a mansion where he could entertain his growing number of leaders from around the world or creating a charitable foundation that could touch the lives of millions of people Herbalife may not reach directly, everything he truly wanted to happen, did happen!

"Do not wait for leaders - do it alone person to person"
Mother Teresa

He employed this essential success quality like the master creator he was in leading the way with an - *anything is possible* - attitude, which he always backed up by demonstration.

Mark always actualized what he said he would. It was never just motivational talk to him. If he said Herbalife would do something, he followed through with his promise. Relaxed, focused intensity was typical of Mark

Mark understood the power of a clear focused thought, and the even greater power of many people concentrating on the same clear focused thought. No sooner had Herbalife reached a particular level of sales and expansion than Mark would raise the corporate bar to a new height that virtually everyone thought was too high.

Before the crowd could debate the wisdom of the goal, Mark would launch into a detailed plan of how he intended to accomplish this new height. One of his most effective techniques for drawing the minds of his distributors up to the level he was already focused on was through repetition of a single word or phrase.

"Only those who risk going too far
can possibly find out how far they can go"
T.S. Elliot

One particular target stands out in my memory. In the early 90's Herbalife had made an amazing recovery from the downturn caused by the challenges in the 80's. Mark got $1 billion in sales into his mind and fixed it there like a bulldog with a bone. When he first launched the goal at a major event he must have said the phrase $1 Billion over a hundred times during his motivational speech.

Mantra - Slogans By the time we all left the stadium we could hear nothing else but the $1 billion slogan playing like a mantra, collectively echoing in our minds. The focused intensity of thousands of us mentally chanting the $1

Billion mantra-slogan completely overshadowed anything else Mark may have said during his talk. *Walked and talked...the same walk and talk.*

128

*"If you knock long enough and loud enough at the gate,
you are sure to wake up somebody"*
Henry Wadsworth Longfellow

I know everyone of us left with the unshakable belief the new target would occur. And of course it did, not on Mark's original schedule, but it did happen because the powerful mantra-slogan continued until Universal Mind finally complied.

Mark was just as tenacious about finding and fostering the dreams of his distributors as he was about his own dream because he knew the one would help fulfill the other.

"The greatest good you can do for others is not just to share your riches but to reveal their own (riches to them)"
Benjamin Disraeli

At one leadership weekend training the #1 distributors at the time, John and Susan Peterson had taken their mid-day break and gone out and purchased an expensive yacht. When Mark heard about it he seized the opportunity to fan the flames of this dynamic young couple's dreams.

"I think I aughta lock up John and Susan on the Shamwars (his 17 million dollar luxury ship) until they start to REALLY shoot high."

Naturally the crowd went wild. Mark was not saying there is never enough, he was taking a unique moment and inspiring his distributors to *reach beyond their grasp*, to be the best they could be in every situation. Mark knew that the toys and accomplishments were merely the records of the levels already achieved.

In the thousands of testimonies about distributors' accomplishments that I ever heard, the most frequent tag line was *"I can't believe I achieved _____."* On a subconscious level, this statement is never true.

"Whatever the mind of man/woman
can conceive and believe, it can achieve."
Napoleon Hill

Without the conception of the idea or dream, the eventual attainment of it is impossible. Mark knew that the conscious mind sends programs to the subconscious mind that is the factory, and delivers to us what we request. He understood the power of *repetition of a powerful image* to bring about change and manifest dreams.

He knew that once he set the die in place, it would stamp out the image into physical manifestation. This simple concept was one of the reasons Mark was able to adapt to so many situations and create the concepts that were needed in the moment.

He merely *allowed* the power within himself (and all of us) combined with the image set in the subconscious mind, and the results came forth effortlessly. This does not mean without action, it means without struggle.

Mark created or inspired other mantra/slogans that are still in use in Herbalife today and are often imitated by other companies:

~Seize the Moment~

~Lose Weight Now - Ask Me How~

~First, Spiritual Life, then Family Life, after that Herbalife~

~Drink and Shrink~
(*that's one of mine*)

~Simply the Best~
(borrowed from Tina Turner's song)

~If you hang around the flag-pole long enough, you will succeed~

Summary

Thought creates everything

1-   nothing just happens, everything began with a thought

2-   therefore, all change in our world requires a change in our thought

Intuition
and
Creativity

"He who looks outside - dreams.
He who looks inside - awakens"
Carl Jung

Mark definitely had his own unique drum beat. He improved on what was good which got him into the ballpark, but when he stepped up to the plate he hit the ball like no other player

The Link To Miracles

"Common sense is intuition. Enough of it is genius"
George Bernard Shaw

Intuition We have touched on the subject of intuition several times because it is the conduit through which our life purpose flows, together with the instruction manual for its achievement.

Simply put, the mind has three basic levels - the logical mind, the abstract mind and the highest, the intuitive mind. Most of mankind has focused on the first two levels until the latter part of the 20th century. This resulted in an *out there* attitude toward creativity. Its basic premise said *if we do certain things a certain way, then this or that will happen.*

"In the hour of your need it will be given unto you"
Matthew 6:33

On close examination of the historical formulas for creating results of any kind we will find that these formulas have constantly changed. What was true yesterday does not apply today. However, Universal Mind is precise and completely reliable. What is true today was true at the time of the big bang and will remain so for eternity.

The Shift Inward As we mentioned in an earlier chapter, there is a shift now occurring which is redirecting our focus from *outside* to *inside.* As we said, in the field of personal development, the shift is moving from motivation to inspiration. We have stated that motivation is an outside-in concept that necessitates a hands-on approach that utilizes books, tapes, videos, CD's, workshops and counseling.

As we redirect our focus inward, we begin to stimulate the highest or intuitive aspect of the mind which is linked to Universal Mind. This expression of mind recognizes no external authority. The inspiration that comes to us from this focus arrives pure and unencumbered by the *rose-colored glass* effect of another's opinion.

---

*"There is guidance for each of us (individually)
and by (humble) listening we shall hear the right words"*
Ralph Waldo Emerson

While there is real value in the influence of motivation to lead us to the trough of inspiration, we must ourselves drink of its creative elixir in order to benefit thereby. Once we have tasted of its pristine drought, we will never again be satisfied with and rely on outside sources for our sustenance. We will be drawn back more and more often to the only true source of abundant life, the True source of creativity, Universal Mind.

This link to Universal Mind, to our true-life purpose, this ever-present joy, has always been available to us and is ours for the asking. However until recently most people have been content to take tiny sips of this miraculous water as it comes to them through fleeting moments of insight, hunches and flashes of inspiration - which they frequently ignore. Often, when a flash of truth comes to pass it is frequently referred to as; *"Hindsight is 20/20."*

Most people then return to the old horse-and-buggy methods to achieve their desires when a limousine and chauffeur is sitting in their driveway waiting for their instructions of where they want to go.

Allowing How do we tap into this telephone line to God, to Universal Mind? How do we link our mind to the ultimate source of all creativity so that the ways and means of achieving our dreams will be constantly and instantly available to us?

Allowing is the first requisite. The telephone line already exists within us but we rarely pick up the phone consciously. It does fall off its cradle occasionally, flashing its messages to us automatically in moments of high emotion such as is the case with emergencies and times of great excitement, but this can hardly be acceptable when we finally recognize its invaluable gifts.

Faithfulness The second step is faithfulness. We need to accept the possibility that this connection actually exists and simply ask It for Its gifts of guidance, inspiration and creative ideas.

It is waiting for us to open the door and invite It into our life. And It will bring far more to us than we ask It for because it knows exactly what we need for our highest purpose, when we need It, and will go on to provide it for us in ways that often seem miraculous.

"Behold, I stand at the door and knock..."
Revelation 3:20

Once we begin to carry on a constant dialogue with this flawless source of guidance, it will quickly become apparent that creative imagination flows effortlessly to us. We are given as many ideas as we can handle, all in perfect accord with our highest purpose.

And, there is a ripple effect that spreads with increasing momentum to everyone we touch and who are receptive to it. Soon we will begin to see that everyone and everything is reflecting what we have become.
People feel inspired just to be around our dream and us. There is an unseen force that excites and invigorates

everything in our path and we will find things fall into place with amazing ease.

> *"You must be the change you wish to see in your world"*
> **Mahatma Gandhi**

Challenges, when they do occur, are easily dealt with and the number of balls we are able to juggle at one time will seem to be infinite. To get a feel for this incredible joy filled state, imagine the myriad activities the body carries on without your conscious awareness and often in spite of your reckless treatment of it.

The same source that carries out these essential activities without your help is the source that is available to your conscious request for guidance. We need only follow Its perfect guidance as it comes to us and It will do the rest. It will find the path of least resistance for each and every thing that needs to happen in order for our dreams to come true.

> *"It is the heart (intuition) always that sees,*
> *before the head can see"*
> **Thomas Carlyle**

Gratitude The last requisite is *gratitude.* Giving thanks is an act of humble recognition. It recognizes that there is a source greater than ourselves that exists within us and around us. It is through this act of thanksgiving that we literally open the channel to this power source, that part of our divinity that creates all of our dreams *out of Itself.*

It is constantly flowing through us and is available to us at all times because we are part of It, we are one with it. It heals the false wound of separation that has taken the ocean's power from the droplet of water and reunites us into the awareness of our wholeness with All that Is. This reality was always there but through our free will we blocked it believing that we could be separate from It. We cannot be separate from It, but we can temporarily believe that we are separate from It. Remember,

---

"As we believe, so it is unto us."
Matthew 21:22

These are the keys to tapping into our intuitive link with Universal Mind. Allow the guidance to come to and through us, be faithful to Its direction and be constantly in gratitude for the gifts It brings to us, everything else will be added unto to us,

Thinking Outside the Box

"Imagination is more important than logic"
Albert Einstein

A Unique Drum Beat Every great leader marches to a different drummer, his own mystifying rhythm. He or she thinks outside the box of conventional thinking and is a source of what becomes the next generation of conventional thinking. *The fad that becomes the trend that becomes the norm* is a common occurrence for creative leadership.

Mark definitely marched to a different drummer; one that mystified even those who knew him for years. He improved on what was good which got him into the ballpark, but when he stepped up to the plate he hit the ball like no other player.

Home run pitches were the only balls he went for and like Babe Ruth, he struck out more than most other players but he also hit many more out of the park than most other players did, so many, that home runs were his claim to fame. The strikeouts weren't even considered.

Necessity Nurtures Invention Once when a particularly offensive water filtration company was making headlines, many neophyte distributors, thinking short term and having little to lose by jumping ship, joined the ill fated company. And many new prospective distributors who might have joined Herbalife went in the same direction. Mark's creative reply was to add a water filtration division to Herbalife, supplied by the highest quality manufacturer available at the time. Mark's focus was always on the safest and highest quality products.

When the disreputable water Filtration Company was put out of business by the authorities, Mark simply allowed the new division to fade away. No big hula-balu was made. He simply and creatively made available to his distributors what they thought they would find in this other company's product. Ultimately this creative concept saved many customers and distributors the loss of their money, their opportunity and exposure to an unsafe product.

Mark knew that the passion he had for his dream was the nucleus around which his distributors and staff would build their own dreams. When they explored their own life purpose, they too would find their own unique passion, which would be directed toward their own dream. Mark's dream would become their *vehicle* for achieving it.

However, in order to motivate the maximum focus and energy toward his dream, he first and foremost sold himself.

Believing in Another's Belief Everyone bought Mark first and his dream, and Herbalife second. They first *believed in his belief.* Any self doubt that they may at first have, was overcome by the contagious enthusiasm, confidence and unfailing passion Mark always exhibited for his dream.

"That which we love, we come to resemble"
St. Bernard of Chairvaux

This was truly a stroke of creative genius and could only have been acted out as an extension of an inner guided direction. Mark would frequently, humorously but humbly refer to himself as, *"Your fearless leader."*

Over-The-Top Image It was a superman parody that worked. What Mark imagined, planned, promoted and absolutely believed in was always over-the-top, even for the most expansive dreamers.

He was a role model that rivaled a super-hero. His designer clothing, his mansions, his fleet of luxury automobiles, his luxury cruise boats, his gala parties and extravaganza's...everything he did was larger than life and was used to provide the model his team needed to meet the challenge of his dream, while fulfilling their own.

It was a constant creative challenge for him to out-do himself, to top himself so that others would follow suit and speed easily behind the wake of his passion.

Creative Brainstorming Mark had an antenna for creative brainstorming. You could see his attention become riveted when he *smelled* a potentially good idea.

In the midst of a huge event with thousands of people and a detailed agenda, if he heard an idea from the audience, or on a break, he would quickly incorporate it into the day's schedule so that he could get feedback and develop the idea among the many other creative minds present. If it seemed to make sense and there was a consensus of agreement concerning its validity, we would see it blend in to the company structure very soon thereafter.

Mark's genuine encouragement of creativity naturally motivated hundreds of ideas to flow into the company. As a result, an entire department was set up just to receive *ideas.*

"Don't play what's there, play what's not there"
Miles Davis

On one occasion, I went for a midnight swim at a beautiful Maui resort in which I was attending a leadership weekend. Several other distributors had the same idea and very soon we all ended up in a hot tub where we spent over an hour brainstorming.

When I told Mark about it the next day he looked disappointed that he had missed the impromptu creative get-together and with genuine interest asked me to please call him next time. I was slightly surprised at first but when I thought about it I realized he never minimized any opportunity to nurture his dream with fresh concepts.

Summary

Perfect creating is guided from within

1-   our "intuition" is the connection to the perfect guidance of the Universal Mind within us

2-   cultivating this connection insures that we will always be on track with our life purpose

3-   we accomplish this through allowing, faithfulness and gratitude

Gratitude

---

*"Love cannot be far behind a grateful
heart and a thankful mind"*
A Course in Miracles

Mark Hughes walked with an incredible posture of expectancy. He wielded the power of gratitude in every area of his life

Giving and Receiving are One

"An attitude of gratitude creates blessings"
Sir John Templeton

Basic Quantum Physics Basic quantum physics tells us that through *the information of our thoughts* combined with the *wave energy within the infinite field of all possibilities,* sometimes referred to as, *The Quantum Soup, a particle forms.* Provided we keep our focus steadily upon it, the thought must and will expand and manifest fully in our world.

With this understanding great power becomes available to us. It was always there, but being unaware of it we may have casually thrown out our thoughts with little or no concern about what may come of them. As a result many of them dissipated from lack of attention.

The Field of Infinite Possibilities This field of infinite possibilities is Universal Mind - All that Is. *It creates everything from Itself.* There is nothing outside It since It could not be One if that were possible.

When we think a thought, and hold our mind steadily on that thought with a sense of expectancy or faith, it must come into physical manifestation. That manifestation arrives out of the infinite field of all possibilities which prior to our thought was only a *hazy wave of potential.*

Understanding the power that exists within our mind to create what we desire also requires that we become aware of and utilize what comes after its creation - gratitude. Gratitude is far more than thanking The Great Source of the fulfillment of our desires, it is knowing that when we think of a desire and affirm that it will be in our life by giving thanks for it, we are using our divine power to decree or co-create with God.

"When I was a child I thought as a child...when I (grew up in understanding) I put away childish things"
1 Corinthians 13:11

Here is an example: *"I am now enjoying a 4,000 square foot mountainside home. It has a spectacular view overlooking the ocean. I feel warm, cozy and affluent. The date is 20__(future date). I give thanks that it is done now."*

By this simple statement, we are affirming that in the realm of thought, we are thankful that it is done now. This statement is the key to the concept of belief or faith, and belief is essential for us to bring about any condition we desire. Whether it is the preparation of dinner, the acquisition of dream home or peace of mind.

The gratitude precedes the visible manifestation of our desire because to Universal Mind, when we affirm or decree a thing, it is already done. And provided we keep our steady, faithful focused attention on the thought we have affirmed that it will manifest in our world.

Gratitude and Expectation Why is gratitude so important? *Because it establishes a sense of worthiness in us.* When we feel worthy we expect to receive what we have asked for. Lack of worthiness is the greatest cause of poverty in the world. If we are taught that we are not good enough to receive or if we tell ourselves that what we have thought and said and done in life disqualifies us for certain kinds of reward, we close the door to our good, to receiving our heart's desires.

"If you have faith of a mustard seed and say to the
mountain move, it will move"
Matthew 17:20

Giving thanks, before we see our desire appear, establishes a state of expectancy. We must hold out the cup for it to be filled. *This is not begging, this is anticipating.* If we want to fly from Miami to London we go to the Miami airport, report in at the flight desk and check our luggage.

Then we go to the gate and wait for the announcement to board. When the call to board is made we get on board and take our seat in full expectation that soon we will land in London. Our expectation is fulfilled because we believe it will be.

Gratitude and expectancy go hand in hand because giving and receiving are one. The great giver of All that Is, is just that - a Giver.

"For God so loved the world, that he gave"
John 3:16

Giving and Receiving Are One As we have repeatedly stated Universal Mind or God is One, and because It is One, It knows that It can only give to Itself. The giving and receiving occur at one and the same moment, the *manifestation of the giving* has nothing whatever to do with *that fact.* This is because the process of fulfillment of creation begins the moment the thought to create it is made.

This is the moment you need to give thanks and this establishes that the Creation is done. And again, gratitude is part of the process to open the channel to your link with Universal Mind.

To give to ourselves is to love ourselves, the true Self that is One with Universal Mind. And love is the primary essence of Universal Mind. Loving our- Selves therefore, is loving our Creator. Self love is by definition is:

"a profound sense of worthiness."

Therefore when we give to our-Selves, we are actually thanking our Universal Self; we are acknowledging that we deserve to receive. Being in a constant state of gratitude places us in the flow of giving (creating) and receiving and validates our understanding of the power we possess in thought to create.

A Life of Gratitude

"Your active exertions are due not only to society, but in humble gratitude to the Being who made you a member of it, with powers to serve yourself and others"
Walter Scott

Always Giving Back Mark Hughes walked with an incredible posture of expectancy. He wielded the power of gratitude in every area of his life. And the rewards validated that power well beyond the material things he and his company received.

After the 2nd surge of business began in the 90's, Mark sought out many distributors who had departed during the storms of the mid 80's and urged them to come back into the fold. He would tell them with absolute certainty, *"You're not even gonna believe what's gonna happen..."* To substantiate his prophecy he would offer the wayward distributor his or her check back.

What that meant to the distributors in question was that the monthly *"royalty"* income that they would have received from the business they left behind would be returned to them...along with all the growth that had occurred since they departed.

"The measure of a man's character is what he would do if he was never found out"
Thomas Macauley

In one case that I am personally aware of, the check approached six figures per month. Mark did not have to offer this to the wayward distributor but he was acutely aware of the contribution that distributor had made to the company previously and wanted to show his gratitude.

In those years many people returned to the company and brought back with them the skills, experience and new found dedication that helped take Herbalife around the world and fulfill Mark's dream.

"Though I have faith, so that I could remove mountains, and have not charity, I am nothing"
1 Corinthians 13:1

Mark did things like this quietly and where possible, anonymously because he understood how the law of gratitude worked. It is a law that is also known as tithing. He understood that the giving of gratitude in its many forms was giving to himself, to his dream. His phenomenal success through to the achievement of his dream proved beyond any doubt that gratitude yields a harvest well beyond the giving.

Mark's dream, was in itself a gift of gratitude to the world. As we outlined earlier, when the lions came to the door, Mark could easily have cashed out and saved himself a heart wrenching battle. But he knew what gifts he had been given and wanted to show his appreciation by sharing it with everyone that wished to receive. To Mark that meant the entire planet.

So great was his faith and passion in this dream that he took many risks to bring it to fruition as quickly as possible. A company with sales of about $3 billion dollars a year may sound very large, but when those sales are spread over 65 countries it tells a different story.

There are considerable challenges in running an international operation where languages, ingredients, marketing systems and labeling laws vary widely. Customs and ways of doing business are like day and night from one end of the world to another and are very expensive to set up and maintain.

> *"Gratitude is not only the greatest of virtues, but the parent of all the others"*
> **Cicero**

The level of growth Mark's company achieved was spread very thinly around the globe and market share had not even scratched the surface. This rapid global expansion was risky, took great courage and was founded on a desire to give to the entire world the gift of a great dream.

> *"Leap and the net will appear"*
> **Julius Camela**

The world of instant mass communication exposes us intimately every day to the appallingly poor conditions in the area of nutrition and economy all over the world. Mark's dream offered one solution for both concerns. In passionately promoting his dream and carrying the spirit of it around the globe, Mark showed the world his appreciation for what he had been given, As he extended his loving thankfulness, the law of gratitude poured ever greater rewards upon him and his dream.

Summary

Gratitude promotes worthiness to receive

1-   expressing gratitude after focusing thought on your desire sets up a state of expectancy that the manifestation of it will occur

2-   expectancy is a state of faith that something will occur

3-   expectancy also implies a state of worthiness, which is essential for receiving

Love
and
Compassion

"Someday, after mastering winds, waves, tides and gravity, we shall harness the energy of love; and for the second time in the history of the world, man will have discovered fire."
Pierre Teilhard de Chardin

Every meeting Mark conducted ended with him saying: "...and may God bless every single one of you." You could feel his passion that indeed, everyone would be blessed.

Love in Action

*"Your work can be called successful only when in
some way it serves your fellow-man"*
Paramahansa Yogananda

Everything is Made of Love On first blush the concept of love and big business seem like strange bedfellows. Our natural tendency might be to say there is no love in business and commerce, only competition and a pervasive attitude of looking-out-for-number-one.

Those things actually exist in business, however we may wish to examine the nature of love before being too quick to judge the lack of it in business. We have already alluded to the fact that in many cultures and spiritual beliefs, God is referred to as *being One or Oneness.*

Each of these beliefs also refers to *God and Love* as being synonymous. To briefly continue our discussion on quantum physics, best selling author Dr. Deepak Chopra, an authority on science, medicine and spirituality, has stated in his many books, tapes and seminars that everything that exists is made up of *energy and information.* He has outlined that science has proven that in the un-manifest condition, everything is *in a wave state of infinite possibilities* in a field of *infinite possibilities.*

Universal Mind is Neutral What is really fascinating is the fact that the wave only becomes a particle when we place our attention on it. Our intention *impregnates* the wave with the requisite information to bring forth the visible manifested form. It literally *creates our intention out* of the energy potential of Itself. Of Itself, it is neither positive nor negative, It simply flows into the pattern or mold we have set for it by our most predominate focused thoughts.

If we really comprehend the power we have because of this truth, this information is overwhelming. Strictly interpreting the two compatible ideas that God is One and God is Love, we must arrive at the inevitable conclusion that everything that is created out of this quantum soup of waves of nothingness and information is made Love. Therefore, the essence of everything, including seemingly *negative* things, is Love.

It may be hard to visualize the idea that our bills are made of Love, or a ghetto is formed out of Love or our worst enemy is made of Love. Nevertheless, these and every other manifested person place thing or circumstance is made of Love.

"Love is its own reward"
Thomas Merton

We may be tempted to look at our world through the judging physical eyes and find much of it distasteful, uncomfortable and even ugly, but this does not in any way take away from the underlying love component that makes it visible to us. To get a clear understanding of this we need to add another ingredient, *free will.*

We may use water to bath in, to nourish our bodies or to mix with other ingredients to produce a new and useful form. We may also flood our basement with it or drown in it. The water itself is neutral, as is the entire universe, the un-manifested field of infinite possibilities.

Let us apply this concept to business, which includes every physical condition, person, circumstance and daily activity. Every one of these is built out of the building blocks of Love. If allowed to follow Its divine course, this essential building block will effortlessly (this does not mean without labor) produce abundance, harmony and joy for all it touches.

Where we get stuck is when we interfere with the natural flow that Love always seeks. Let's examine that flow and see where it would go if not interfered with.

Wholeness A primary characteristic of Love is Wholeness, since it is One with All that Is, God or Universal Mind. Remember, God is One and God is love, therefore Love is also One. This means that *Love flows in the direction of unity* not division, separation or conflict.

All Inclusiveness In seeking Wholeness, all are treated equally, all receive the same Wholeness since Wholeness must mean Oneness. Therefore, Wholeness is all-inclusive.

"God (Love or Universal Mind) is no respecter of persons."
Acts 10:34

Abundance Wholeness also suggests completeness or an over-flow of everything that is needed. A state of being filled with abundance without need of any kind. To go with the flow of Love is to be Whole, complete and abundant in every sense of the word. Naturally, this abundance would include material needs, relationships and health. The Wholeness of Love therefore heals all lack.

Service Love, being One can only give Itself to Itself. As a result, Love must be constantly giving and receiving in the same moment, in an unbroken chain of moments. To serve is to go with the flow of giving, however it also means to receive in equal measure.

Oneness is a circle of giving and receiving and to take an ascetic attitude of giving without allowing Love to give back is to separate us from the flow of Oneness. While we may temporarily block our receiving, we cannot indefinitely prolong it returning to us because there is nothing outside Love, it must return to itself eventually. Blocking our good constricts the flow of the natural of Law of Love and in turn causes constriction in our lives on every level that we experience.

Forgiveness Allows Love to Flow The healing power of love has been witnessed in many well-documented cases in which prayer and compassion were extended. People laden with physical blockages such as arthritis, heart conditions (that arose from constricted blood flow) or respiration difficulties were returned to a state of Wholeness. In our own work we have seen many people transformed from physical disease to wellness when they allowed themselves to be loved.

"There is no difficulty that enough Love will not conquer"
Emmet Fox

How can Love be accepted as the healer that is it? The answer is:

When people forgive themselves.

Guilt is the single greatest cause of blocking the flow of Love due to the sense of unworthiness it creates. When we forgive ourselves we allow the highest good or Love to return to our bodies, our finances, our relationships and our world.

Using these truths as a template, let us overlay them onto the world of business and commerce. When we believe that in offering our products and services to the world, we are really offering them to ourselves, our thoughts, words, deeds and service will be in accord with the immutable law of Love and will prosper along with everyone and everything we touch.

The Spirit of Mark's Dream

"Intense love does not measure, it just gives."
Mother Teresa

Profiled - Love Although Herbalife is primarily a natural health company underpinned by the natural healing enhancement of herbs, weight loss has always been its calling card. The theory behind this is both clever and logical. Weight loss is a highly emotional subject.

Many people will do and have done just about anything to lose weight, often dangerous, unhealthy things. As a result, getting a new customer to try Herbalife products from a weight loss perspective first is rather easy.

However, once a person begins to actually FEEL the positive difference in her health, she want to know WHY. Then the distributor simply TELLS the customer the nutritional reasons why they are feeling good while they are losing weight, instead of trying to SELL them.

It's a two step approach that is gentle and requires a simple belief and understanding in the products but no special marketing ability. It works, and virtually anybody can do it. That was Mark's plan; give everybody a fun, simple and magical way to get people using the products. When they feel good, they will stay on the products.

To highlight the products, which is the foundation of Herbalife's success on a tangible level, testimonials are paraded across stages all around the world in every meeting, large or small.

> *"They do not love that do not show their love"*
> **Shakespeare**

Whenever Mark conducted this part of a training event, which he loved to do, you could see him standing off to one side of the stage, often in the shadows, watching as each person told their emotional story.

Since I was in the top level of the company's distributors, I usually sat toward the front of the stage at these events. It was normal for me and everyone else nearby to see tears streaming down Mark's face as life changing testimonies were shared one after the other. There were no TV monitors on Mark at the time; the audience and cameras were focused on the speakers.

> *"Love is the subtlest force in the world"*
> **Mahatma Gandhi**

His emotion was completely genuine and heartfelt. Every meeting Mark conducted ended with him saying: *"...and may God bless every single one of you."* You could feel his passion that indeed; everyone would be blessed.

> *"Joy is the serious business of Heaven"*
> **T. S. Elliot**

Focused Love One time in the late 80's I was attending a special Leadership conference in Maui with Mark. There were perhaps 35 of us at the time as it was just as the company was coming out of its *dark night* .

During this time, while I waited for the company to turn the corner I had taken a part time job while continuing to perform my duties as a distributor with the company. Mark was cultivating the distributors he felt could help him lead the company into the next decade that he knew would be explosive and had gathered us together at his estate on the beautiful Hawaiian Island.

During that time Mark asked me to take a stroll around his estate with him. He put his arm around my shoulder, and despite his being ten years younger than me, it felt like the loving guidance of an older brother.

He explained to me his vision for the future and his need for key people to take the company to the next level and all the while made me feel as though I was the most special person he had ever met.

That was one of Mark's greatest assets, he focused his attention completely on the person right in front of him no matter what distractions there may have been around him at the moment.

"To do two things at once is to do neither"
Publilius Syrus

Another time Mark was standing in a reception line at his famous Beverly Hills mansion called *Gray hall.* It was a black tie event and everyone was decked out in their finest. A busload of distributors had just been dropped off and the front foyer of the grand entranceway was jammed with starry-eyed guests. Everyone vied for Mark's attention but he had his attention riveted on one particular distributor he was speaking with.

As I was standing nearby I overheard the conversation which was basic small talk. However, Mark gave that person the precious gift of himself, no less than if he was the President of the United States discussing world policy with the heads of state.

Compassion On yet another occasion partially discussed in an earlier section, Mark threw a Gala party in a tent beside a small lake on the outskirts of Orlando, Florida. It was another black tie event with virtually all the top distributors and staff in Herbalife at the time. The buses dropped us off at the beginning of what felt like an endless red carpet winding down and around a steep hill and finally up to the entrance of the huge white canvas structure.

"A human being is part of a whole, called by us the 'Universe,' a part limited in time and space. He experiences himself, his thoughts and feelings, as something separated from the rest - a kind of optical delusion of his consciousness. This delusion is a kind of prison for us, restricting us to our personal desires and to affection for a few persons nearest us. Our task must be to free ourselves from this prison by widening our circles of compassion to embrace all living creatures and the whole of nature in its beauty."
Albert Einstein

We were greeted at the tent by white-gloved butlers holding trays of Dom Peringnon. We were then seated at tables, dazzling with the finest crystal and silver circling beautiful ice sculptures and adorned with dozens of roses. An orchestra played Mozart in one corner, a magician dazzled us in another corner and a wandering photographer popped paparazzi shots for future corporate promotions. We heard later that Patti Labelle was scheduled to show up on a hovercraft outside the tent after dinner and entertain us.

Everything seemed heavenly. *All of a sudden, there was a soul-piercing scream!* I looked around and saw a half dozen horrified people at a nearby table struggling to get to their feet. Their table had dropped into a deep indentation in the floor that had appeared without warning.

It seems that the Gala organizers had unknowingly built the tent on a sinkhole and the entire structure was threatening to disappear along with the company, at any moment. Pandemonium broke out.

Within minutes the dauntless Mike McKee, now VP of marketing was imitating an airline parking engineer and calmly waving everyone to the exit.

As I headed to safety along with the rest of the crowd I noticed Mark, almost hidden behind the bandstand. He was holding Jacque Lueth, the corporate executive responsible for creating the evening's spectacular vent. She had broken down in uncontrollable weeping, filled with guilt.

One would think Mark would be the first to be whisked away from the impending demise of the facility. Instead he was gently and compassionately consoling the distraught employee.

It was a rare opportunity to witness openly what occurred frequently in private. Mark was the father figure, patron, inspirer, comforter and to some people, nick of time saint, more frequently then not, unknown to almost everyone but the recipient.

Perhaps the incident that moved me the greatest was just after Mark returned form a grueling cross country tour of investment and financial institutions. These companies control large funds and since Herbalife was listed on Nasdaq, Mark had been promoting his company to them. Success with these people would mean a giant influx of money for his ambitious expansion plans.

At the reception, the evening of my arrival, Mark took the stage beside the orchestra for a few moments and I could not believe my eyes. I had never seen Mark look so wasted. He took a moment to explain why he looked so tired then opened his arms wide as if to embrace the whole room and said.

"I've never seen anything look so good in my whole life...you guys are my family...I love every single one of you."

"Love brings harmony and order out of chaos"
Molly Haskil

After years of these kinds of personal observations, *I believe Mark Hughes was inspired by much more than he knew.* His vision to change the nutritional and financial habits and conditions of the world only scratched the surface of a much deeper commitment to this planet. Of necessity, his attention was focused on his dream in a very down-to-earth material way, but what drove his vision was an innate connection with the highest aspect of his spirit - Love.

---

*"We can do no great things –
only (many) small things with great love"*
Mother Teresa

He loved his dream, he loved his distributors, he loved the customers whose lives had been changes in a myriad ways, he loved his Herbalife family, he loved the world and he loved life - and lived it to the fullest. The heart, the spirit, the essence of his dream was love. If one is inclined to judge, he need only judge a man by his works to get an accurate picture of *"what sleeping giant was awakened within his breast."*

The loving evidence of The Hughes Legacy swells with every wave that ripples from the center of the dream he began February 1st, 1980.

"Listen gang, let me tell you the most important thing to do to make your business grow: "You've got to love and care more about your distributors and customer's success than you do about your own. If you do that the rest will take care of itself."

Summary

Attention on love awakens the condition of abundance

1-   Universal Mind is One or Whole, its essence is Love

2-   focus on Love therefore, is a focus on Wholeness

3-   Wholeness is all-inclusive, it is an abundance of everything seen and unseen.

World Service

"He profits most who serves best"
**Arthur F. Sheldon-
Motto for Rotary International**

Perhaps more than anything else in his life, Mark Hughes understood the universal law of Cause and Effect - "what goes around comes around"

Cause and Effect

"Service is love made manifest"
Maharishi Sadashiva Isham

Truth- The Changeless Law Truth is frequently a question of enforced honesty and morality. This brand of honesty is often fueled by subtle societal fear. *'You better watch out, you better not pout, cuz....'* This negative motivation applies to things many people think they can't get away with.

"What you sow, so shall you reap."
Galatians 6:7

We have been told that if we sow cheating, lying, stealing and injury to others, that eventually we will find that reaping a whirlwind of similar effects is not worth the risk. This kind of zealous encouragement to *'be good or else'* has filled the pews of many religious structures for centuries. To a point, it has served a worthy purpose and helped civilize a world that might otherwise have long ago destroyed itself through anarchy and self indulgence.

However, when taken too far, it breeds a slowly brewing resentment because fear, and its entire offspring, is the opposite of love, and love is the foundation of Truth. How then does genuine love take root in your heart?

First, it must be self initiated, unhindered by outside coercion.

"Our greatness lies not so much in being able to remake the world as in being able to remake ourselves"
Mahatma Gandhi

167

Understanding the changeless, unfailing law of cause and effect, the precise reaping of what you sow, is a good beginning, but for love to be authentic, more is required.

Love One Another This is not merely an expansion of the ten Mosaic laws of civilization. It is a scientific law, which clearly understands the Oneness of mankind within the Oneness of Universal Mind.

"Thou shalt love thy neighbor as thyself"
Leviticus 19:18

If this be true, *what and for that matter, where could anything else exist.* It is both logical and reasonable to accept the fact that we must be part of that One or Oneness.

As we have already pointed out, most cultures believe that God is Love. Is it possible then for God to be sometimes hateful, cruel, revengeful and indulge in special relationships, giving good to some that It favors and taking away from those It does not? If God is love and God is One, then It can only *be loving* Itself. *How then could It possibly love Itself unequally?*

"The Lord our God is One!"
Deuteronomy 6:4

If we are One with the Oneness of Universal Mind, we too must, at our core, also be love. The root of living in truth must then be to love all, ourselves and all life - our world. To sow this seed is to reap a whirlwind of joy. We must nourish our garden with love, which is the entire world, not just our small circle of family and friends.

In this way, when the harvest time comes, we will not be disappointed. This harvest is not in some far off ephemeral paradise but here and now. The effects of our thought word and deed manifests in every moment.

"Every action in our lives touches some chord that will vibrate into eternity"
Edwin Hubbel Chapin

When we practice living in love, which includes all our activities, all our thoughts and all our words extended to all life, we activate a principle which is in perfect harmony with the original plan, the First Cause. As result there is not enough room for the bounty, the abundance that will return to us.

Be - Do - Have Most people operate their life through the *Do - Have - Be* principle. They believe that by *doing something,* be it their career, their relationship roles, their community service activities or whatever function that holds their greatest interest, something of value will accrue to them. And in the *acquisition of that something*, they will *be-come* somebody. This process is *fear based* and filled with struggle.

The truth about our role in life is just the reverse. *We are already someone of great value* because we are One with All that Is. We are co-creators with Universal Mind. There is no higher state of being.

From this lofty state we need only follow the highest purpose we have within us and the *doing* becomes effortless. *Having* then, is a bi-product of performing our joy, which is living our truth, our purpose our passion.

Altruism

"God is the Father, Earth is the Mother.
With all things and in all things, we are relatives"
Sioux - Native American

A Citizen of The World Look at a world map which illustrates where Herbalife has a presence. At this writing there are 58 countries in which Herbalife is doing business and serving its citizens.

Mark's goal to take Herbalife, together with its life changing products and opportunity around the world, was fulfilled before his passing in April of 2000. One could almost imagine that his unique life purpose had been fully realized and it was time for him to pass on to greater things.

The physical presence of his dream circling the globe was just the foundation of a loftier dream and perhaps that was his mission. All of us have a unique purpose, a mission, which like a relay runner, is passed on to another generation to take a few steps further before they too pass on the expanding dream to another.

"Those who bring sunshine to the lives of others
cannot keep it from themselves"
James M. Barrie

One thing is for certain, the spirit of Mark's dream lives on in the hearts of millions of people of many cultures, with many beliefs and many levels of understanding of what life means to them. His spirit-dream has been a catalyst that is now joined with these diverse mixtures of life, of love, of family, and of community and is fostering a deeper awareness of what each of their lives and the world can be.

With this higher vision, the united power of a collective awareness cannot fail to influence the world for good. Not just in bodies that are vitally alive with quality nutrition, nor with the power to control one's financial health, but with a heart centered focus that seeks ever to lift his or her fellow man. Mark's dream has provided a vehicle for millions of people around the world to more easily meet the everyday challenges of life. And in the quiet space that remains the soul can seek and find a deeper meaning to life.

Whenever I could, I often took great pleasure in stepping back and observing Mark working with his dream, lovingly molding it like a master craftsman. It was obvious the everyday challenges of running a multi-billion dollar corporation *kept him grounded* most of the time.

But between the lines of his demanding leadership role, in quiet moments of reflection, I know the heartfelt spirit of his dream animated his passion in ways that shone like a searchlight. *"Change the world"* was a phrase constantly on Mark's lips, but what he really meant was:

"Heal the world...make it a better place...the dream we were conceived in...will shine again in grace"
Michael Jackson

At one of the first extravaganzas Herbalife hosted, 4,000 of us noisily took our seats and waited for the festivities to begin. On the stage were several huge white globes hanging from the rafters. At the time Herbalife was in only a handful of countries, but it was typical of Mark to paint a giant picture of what he knew was to come.

The room was dark except for special effects lighting which was set up to make it appear like stars were streaming throughout the room and across the globes. Then a vocalist, with a voice almost exactly like Michael Jackson's began singing Michael's song *"Heal the World."*

Everyone stood up and began swaying their arms above their heads like gently flowing waves of wheat. Within minutes everybody was moving in perfect unison with the music. *It was blissfully surreal.*

Later, as the day rolled on and we took our breaks, a videotape played, showing this opening event. It included close up shots of people after the music stopped and the lights came up. I know all of us were transfixed, for it appeared as though the entire room was full of angels, such was the joy on our faces.

"This is the Spirit of Mark's Dream"

In 1994 Mark Hughes created the Herbalife Family Foundation. It was set up as a separate entity from Herbalife and was designed to help feed, cloth, educate and house children and families. Today this is being accomplished in more than many countries with the creation of the Herbalife International Family Foundation. In addition the Herbalife Family Foundation supports a multitude of charities from around the world. A few examples include:

-D.A.R.E. which helps educate children and teens the world over to stay away from drugs.

In the 90's Mark was honored as Man of the Year by D.A.R.E.

-Casa Herbalife is a Brazilian orphanage, which provides housing for girls at risk. It was built in 1996 and is operated by Foundation donations

-In the Czech Republic hospital waiting rooms for children are being redesigned as play areas at the Chantel Arc.

-Charities in over 60 other countries are also being supported

Summary

Every cause has an identical effect and touches everything in some way

1-   whatever we think, say or do sets into play a ripple effect that in someway touches everything, and sooner or later returns to us

2-   by always allowing love to influence what we put out into our world we are assured that everything that returns to us will be influenced by its power

The Next Step

"The joyfulness of a man prolongeth his days"
Psalms

Mark's canvas was from the beginning vast, so inevitably he made many mistakes.

Unattached Joy

"The infinite is the source of joy"
The Upanishad

Missing Pieces History is laden with great accomplishments tainted by imbalanced power. When grand dreams are envisioned, focused upon and achieved, unless they are supported by complete submission to the higher power back of all creation, eventually they must suffer affliction of some kind.

Universal Mind operates through perfect laws, which must be followed if balance is to persist. Viewed from a distance, the seeds of destruction can easily be seen, but when one stands in the middle of the forest, the trees may look healthy and robust as if they could last forever.

This pure vision can only be accomplished when we are detached from our dreams, when they are mere toys with which we play out our dreams in joy, but which can easily be released without remorse. A tall order you may say, but one which is a prerequisite for genuine peace of mind.

This wise adage may be one of the most least followed while one of the most important we have been taught. It is the difference between being the master of our circumstances rather than their servant.

"Be in the world - not of the world"
John 17:14

Once a person understands the power they have to control how their life unfolds through the focused use of thought, circumstances quickly begin to bend to their command. It is at this point that a critical ball is usually dropped. And that ball is submission to the One Life behind the thought that gives it its power to create.

We must release our control, our free will to Its perfect guidance and all will evolve in perfect harmony and peace. This is why we are told to seek first the *Kingdom of Heaven,* a metaphor for *the wisdom of Universal Mind.* This is both scientific and spiritual since it follows *pure logic* and at the same time contains the fundamental seeds of *spiritual common sense.*

We can have whatever we desire and we can have peace of mind in the process provided we hand over our free will to the Will that is One with Universal Mind. It will insure that what we desire is for our highest purpose and it will provide the ways and means to achieve it, often in mysterious, seemingly miraculous ways.

He Came Close to the Mark

"The powers that be are ordained by God"
Romans 13:1

An Interrupted Dream In these pages you have read how one man, Mark Hughes was scarred by personal tragedy and yet found within himself the necessary virtues to accomplish what few people have been able to replicate in their chosen field. It is a true life *"rags to riches"* saga cut short in the prime of life.

The Hughes Legacy was a life that continues to touch and inspire millions of people worldwide, transformed by the inevitable empowerment of human spirit that results whenever mediocrity is transformed by greatness.

Throughout his meteoric rise to power and his influence on the Wellness industry, lives were indeed changed, far more profoundly than his vision had foreseen. With the aid of Herbalife, and by an inner power he may have only just begun to understand, Mark laid a foundation for change that probed to the depths of human potential. It is change, that seeks to magnify the dim light of integrity shining within all of us some of the time, and for a handful of brave souls, all the time.

Mark Hughes was not a perfect man; he had problems and made mistakes just like all of us. Mark's canvas was from the beginning vast, so inevitably he made many mistakes. But few people have transmuted error into achievement more quickly or more creatively than Mark Hughes has. He always looked, with his infectious smile and laughter, at solutions and made everyone believe they too could do the same.

When he fell down...which he sometimes did, be bounced back...usually higher than before. It was perhaps this quality in him that underlined the spirit of Mark's dream the most.

But the heart of Mark's dream, the essence and spirit of it, was love. Somewhere, in the unfolding process of his dream, the key ingredient to peace of mind was missed and Mark's personal joy was not fully achieved. He reached for and attained the heights of human accomplishment, but missed the golden ring every soul seeks at its core.

He came close to the mark but settled for less than he might have personally achieved. Most of us do not come as close as Mark did nor are we willing to pay the price to reach so high.

It is our heartfelt prayer that Mark now shares in the great joy he has spread throughout this world of dreams and tears and that what seeds he sowed will yield abundant harvests of joy and peace and love for millions of people the world over.

The Inside Plan

*"Things which cannot be overcome when they are taken
together, become easy when taken little by little"*
Plutarch

Most people feel comfortable with a plan. Ask any banker who lends money to business. Without a *business plan* an application for financing would not even be considered. When a person applies for work, one of the first things they expect to be given is a *job description*. It is no different in the organization of a successful life - you need a plan.

The question is who designs the plan?

No special education, expertise or experience is necessary in order to live a successful life. Nevertheless, as valuable as these things are as stepping stones, they can actually become obstacles to truly living a life that is both successful in the material sense as well as in the sense of peace of mind or joy. We have left this dichotomous statement until the last few pages of this book because by now you will have a sense for what we mean.

Let us refer back to the first Chapter on Passion. We have stated that Passion follows the pursuit of our Life Purpose. And our Life Purpose comes from a place deep inside that *nothing outside* can show us. We have said that outside systems such as motivation are valuable to the extent that they can lead us inside, but that from there *we must allow* our truth to come forth in order *to know the what* of our Life Purpose.

The guidance that comes through us as a result of allowing the fountain of truth within us to flow unimpeded by *outside influences* IS THE PLAN that will always yield the perfect results for our Life purpose. This can be a little scary because it is an *'in the moment of your need faith'* that often provides us with only *the next step* when everything that the world has told us, in order to be successful says, "we need to think at least a year ahead, if not five years ahead."

We know for certain that Mark Hughes planned in the traditionally accepted way - well in advance. Notwithstanding, he was also completely flexible and could turn on a dime if he was inspired to do so. The key is to always be in that *allowing frame of mind* that leaves open the door for inner inspiration to direct us to the miraculous moments, moments that often accomplish more in an instant than years of executing well-laid plans can produce.

This is *a little by little process* of beginning within our comfort zone, then reaching beyond our grasp, then finally yielding totally to the guidance that comes from within. We need to make our plans, as many as we desire, but remain open and receptive to the inspirations that are always waiting to come forth from within. Then, as we develop more and more faith and come to believe that *foresight IS also 20/20,* we will begin to trust our moment by moment plans more and more to the guidance from within.

Gradually, even the plans we make well in advance will be those that were given to us from our inner source. As we learn to allow these directions to come through and see that they always work out for the best, we will trust more and more in the process and find that planning far in advance becomes less and less necessary.

This is the highest *Formula for Success* there is...complete abandon of our little will to the perfect Will of the guidance from within, that will lead us unerringly to, and through our Life Purpose, living abundantly in joy every moment.

About the Authors

John McIntosh is a dynamic speaker and has been an entrepreneur and leader in the field of sales management, marketing, training and motivation for 38 years. During that time he worked in the insurance and investment fields and rose to the level of national sales manager in two separate companies. He founded two companies for which he acted as president, and for 25 years has held a senior distributorship with the leader in the Wellness Industry. During his career he has trained thousands of people internationally presenting his material with high energy and conviction based on personal experience and success.

Ananda McIntosh is a remarkable intuitive healer, spiritual counselor, Reiki Master and All - Faith Minister, teaching *"A Course in Miracles"* for the last 13 years. She is also a spiritual channel for beautiful prose and a photographer with a perceptive eye for the spirit within all life. For over 15 years she had a strong background in theater in New York successfully performing virtually every function within the framework of producing a play and used these highly tuned skills to help teach children Self Empowerment. Ananda is also a highly skilled graphic artist.

John and Ananda have written a screenplay and several books, novels, articles, short stories and recorded a CD on the subject of **The Law of Attraction**, which include:

Novels

The Millennium Tablets
Loves Last Dreaming
Towering Angels
Love Beads

Screenplay

Loves Last Dreaming

Self Help

Living Abundantly through Inner Guidance
365 Days of Inner Guidance Inspirations
The Millionaire Maker
The TAO of The Secret
I Know The Secret

Calendar

A Course in Miracles
Perpetual Calendar & Journal

Podcasts

including:

Neville Goddard
Dr. Joseph Murphy
Florence Shovel Shinn
The Secret Bank (LOA)
A Course in Miracles

All available at:

www.LawOfAttractionCenters.com

CD
Attunement to Wealth, Health and Happiness

available at:

www.TheAttunementProgram.net

Contact:

createmiracles@aol.com

Printed in Great Britain
by Amazon

47544242R00106